THE PATH OF THE ELDERS

THE PATH OF THE ELDERS

A MODERN EXPOSITION OF ANCIENT BUDDHISM

ERNEST ERLE POWER

MANOHAR
2021

First published 1928
Reprinted 2021

ISBN 978-93-90729-53-1

Published by
Ajay Kumar Jain *for*
Manohar Publishers & Distributors
4753/23 Ansari Road, Daryaganj
New Delhi 110 002

Printed at
Replika Press Pvt. Ltd.

THE
PATH OF THE ELDERS

A MODERN EXPOSITION OF ANCIENT BUDDHISM

BY

ERNEST ERLE POWER

> "For there is the Path of the Elders and there is the Path of the Gods: leading the one unto Nibbana, the Peace Unshakeable; the other unto Heaven, the Glory Unequalled. But the Glory lasteth not, whereas the Peace abideth for ever and aye."
>
> *From the Book of the Sayings of TSEN-RE.*

THEOSOPHICAL PUBLISHING HOUSE

ADYAR, MADRAS, INDIA

1928

DEDICATED

TO HIM WHO ENABLED ME
TO PRESENT, HOWEVER
INADEQUATELY,
HIS TEACHING

CONTENTS

PREFACE

THE following chapters were written in response to a request from interested friends who had attended a series of lectures I had delivered on the subject during a winter's stay in Boston, for a sequential exposition of Buddhism.

The work stands as it was written at the time, without material changes or additions. It represents a popular and modern discussion of original Buddhism, sometimes called THERAVADA (The Teaching of the Elders) or more often HINAYANA (The Little Vehicle), as distinguished from MAHAYANA (The Great Vehicle).

Roughly speaking, Buddhism falls into these two divisions: the Hinayana (sometimes called Southern Buddhism), referring to the methods of reaching Nibbana by individual exertion and therefore represented as the little vehicle, for each man constructs his own raft upon which to cross the stream of transitory existence; the Mahayana (also called Northern Buddhism), on the other hand, as a collective vehicle for the masses, requiring less individual understanding and effort, and depending more upon the guidance of those who constitute themselves leaders to salvation.

The Hinayanist maintains that the Mahayanist may reach Union with Deity, at-one-ment or yoga: but does not attain Nibbana, for the simple reason that this can only be accomplished by *individual* exertion, and that the Mahayanist, by virtue of adhering to his particular views, has lost the understanding of the true meaning of Nibbana, confusing it with at-one-ment which no doubt he *can* attain. But such attainment, according to the Hinayanist, does not by any means lead the former beyond the necessity for further rebirth and evolution. For the God consciousness to which the Mahayanist aspires, is still the consciousness of a Being impermanent and imperfect, though from the limited human level its impermanency cannot easily be perceived nor its imperfection easily realized.

The Path of the Elders represents Buddhism in its purest and most original form. It is retained mainly in Ceylon, Burma and Siam. Its ethical value has never been surpassed and its philosophical concepts have never been successfully combated.

A great deal of misconception concerning both Buddhist ethics and Buddhist philosophy prevails in Christian countries, due to two peculiar circumstances. The one dates from the period that Buddhist documents were translated into European languages for the first time, when the translators, through lack of adequate material, naturally did not have a clear understanding of Buddhist concepts. We may mention the case of Professor Max Müller who in his earlier writings vigorously maintained that Nibbana stood for annihilation, which opinion he modified a few years before his death. Unfortunately, however, his corrected opinion is hardly ever referred to, whilst all possible capital has been made out of the admittedly incorrect notion that Nibbana meant annihilation, by those who considered it a duty to their religion to put as black as possible a complexion upon the tenets of a non-Christian faith.

The other circumstance is the result of missionary effort to convert, not only the "poor heathen" to the views of his particular sect, but also the mind of the Christian world to the necessity of his work. We hear missionaries tell of the profound darkness enveloping the souls of their prospective converts, and generalize upon social conditions by picturing in coarse outline the lowest social strata in Oriental countries. How would we feel if Buddhist missionaries, returning from the stockyards of Chicago, the underworld of New York, the slums of London, or the apache dens of Paris, told their audiences welcoming their return to their native countries, that these conditions were representative of Christian civilization? The time has arrived when, without fear of disrupting the religious coherence of the West, we may look without prejudice or misrepresentation into the face of the religions of the East.

The Buddhist is not primarily concerned with making converts. His main object is to place before his hearers an outline of his views and then leave it with them for their consideration. If they feel impelled to inquire further or even to adopt Buddhism as the highest expression of ethical and philosophical insight, he will see to it that they have the opportunity to do so. But the impulse must come from within the other. The Buddhist holds out no inducements either of a material or of a spiritual order other than those which must of necessity accompany considerate thinking and hurtless conduct. He does not have to believe in a dogma, to accept a creed, or to save a soul. There is but one dogma in Buddhism and that is that it has no dogma; there is but one creed in Buddhism and that is the creed that we must be humane; there is no soul to save in Buddhism for no soul can ever be lost.

It is with considerable diffidence that these popular studies into the tenets of Buddhism are placed before the public. Written during spare moments of an active and busy life they do not pretend completely to cover the subject in hand, nor to represent the only right exposition of Buddhism. Other interpretations may perhaps be more adequate. But the writer has endeavoured to place before the mind of Western readers, in language couched in modern terms, the essential truths of the ancient Buddhist faith of which he himself is an adherent. In glancing through the subsequent pages may the reader realize that the keynote of Buddhist philosophy is Understanding, and that of Buddhist conduct is Love.

INTRODUCTION

EVER since Buddhism has attracted the attention of the western world attempts have been made to account for its remarkable influence over the human thought of the past and to trace back its lofty morality and perfect simplicity to earlier systems of religion.

Those who give a description of Buddhism invariably regard it as an outgrowth of the centuries of Vedic and Brahmanic thought that preceded it in the country of its origin—India. Without its Brahmanic background Buddhism, it seems, cannot be explained. This theory, however, to a great extent is based upon the fact that Gotama Buddha, the founder of Buddhism, the Wisdom Religion, in the exposition of His teaching, constantly employs the terminology familiar to his Brahmanic listeners.

No one will deny that He has, indeed, made use both of the terminology and of the national background provided by His hearers. Had He employed any other He could have left no impress upon their minds. As one must speak English to an English, French to a French audience; use medical terms when addressing physicians and chemical when chemists, so the Buddha had to speak in Indian imagery to His Indian audiences and use Brahminic terms in the exposition of His philosophy. But not because His philosophy was similar to or an outgrowth of that of the Brahmans amongst whom He taught: as a matter of fact, His line of reasoning was so utterly at variance with that of the philosophers of His day that only by speaking to them in a language they could understand, by using images with which they were familiar, by employing philosophical terms to which they attached a definite meaning, could He ever hope to succeed in winning them from their accustomed modes of thinking, and placing before them His own. Any other method would have been like watering a rock, or planting seeds in a desert, or setting fire to a river!

But His doctrine was distinct; it was, in fact, antagonistic to the ideas prevailing in India at His time, and though in some respects resemblances may be found to exist, they are the resemblances between postulates, never between conclusions. Though people may agree that fire is hot, yet one concludes: "Therefore it is harmful"; and another: "Therefore it is useful." Thus, however much some of the postulates of Brahminical doctrines and Buddhistic teaching may resemble one another, they are used to point to different and even contrary conclusions.

Again there are certain trite sayings which are the property of all ages and which may be regarded almost as fundamental to human thought. Such will be found, with hardly a variation, in every religious or philosophical scripture. The fact that they are quoted does not by any means indicate that the entire book in which they are found is taken from the older writing in which they occur. At most it would show that they were current as proverbs or soothsayings. Thus we find a great many resemblances in the books of the Hindus and the Buddhists; of the Persians and the Christians; of the Jews and the Egyptians; of the Aztecs and the Norsemen; of the Greeks and the Druids. And though in many cases a connection may be assumed or found to exist, usually there is more the recognition of the inherent wisdom in the particular saying that is repeated, than the wholesale adoption of the philosophy or the religion in whose books it is found a few centuries earlier. Thus we may find a number of similar epigrams in Hindu and in Buddhist scriptures—and great stress has been laid upon such resemblances to prove the theory in point—but such sayings as a rule are to be found also in every other literature the world has ever produced.

It is therefore not by any means requisite, in order to get a comprehension of the teachings of the Buddha, to divert our attention preliminarily to whatever thought may have been current in India at the time of the Great Teacher. There is little doubt but that there were at least as many philosophies current in His day as there are in ours, for which reason we may hinge His teaching with as much advantage upon our own modes of thinking as upon any other. There was no uniformity of thought in His day, as little as (if not less than) there is in our times. The man who, a hundred or a thousand years hence, pedantically were to attempt to give an outline of the philosophies and doctrines (and superstitions) prevalent in Europe and America during the nineteenth and twentieth centuries would have before him a task which he could not handle adequately, however much his erudition might be praised by the critics of his time. And when applying this same reasoning to the India of the century preceding Gotama the Buddha, all we need add is that the thinking of those days there, was not only more profound but also much more independent than even ours ! To speak of the philosophy of India 2,500 years ago is like referring to the language of Europe during the reign of Charlemagne, or to the colour of a mosaic. And even as a speech delivered by a man standing upon a chair cannot be the outcome of the fact that he is standing upon that chair—a garden patch, or a table, or a platform might have done just as well—so the teachings of the Buddha, though delivered, as it were, from the mosaic of Indian terminology and simile, are not either their result or their apotheosis: they are independent and unique.

If Buddhism were the direct outcome of Brahmanism, how could we account for its influence in those countries, in thought far removed from Brahmanism, where it is prevalent at this day and where it made itself at home at least as easily as it did in the land of the Veda, the Vedānta, and the Upanishad? Is Christianity the outcome of Judaism? Then how did the doctrine of an eye for an eye suddenly become transformed into that of the Sermon on the Mount? To understand its sublime morality is it necessary to dig up the entire insignificant history of the Jews and make it serve as a post on which to hang the lamp of Christianity? Surely any other post does just as well. Christian morality is accepted by millions who never even heard of Ezra the Scribe, never believed in a jealous and vindictive Jehova, never accepted literally the story of Adam and Eve. Thus it is with Buddhism. The beacon light of the Buddha's Dhamma found an appropriate elevation in the highest level of Indian thought, but any other elevation will serve the purpose.

Having established an Indian mode of thinking, our erudite Indologists calmly proceed to attribute it to climatic conditions, losing sight of the fact that all climates are represented in that wonderful country and that we can speak of "the Indian

B

climate" with about as much consistency as we can of "the Indian mode of thinking"! Moreover, history has shown that Buddhism, though born and developed and matured in those climatic regions which, according to our psychological meteorologists, constituted the very influence favouring such birth and development, after having dominated the thought of the Indian peninsula for some hundreds of years, left its supposedly most congenial soil to flourish still more abundantly and permanently beyond the Himalayan regions in Tibet, Tartary, China, Japan, as well as in Burma, Siam and Ceylon. In view of such facts, what becomes of the climatic theory?

Even the life itself of the great Teacher offers little to account for His phenomenal influence over the thought of mankind. Born and bred in refined and luxurious surroundings, marrying at an early age according to local custom, instructed in the sports and pastimes of His day, receiving His religious instruction most likely at the hands of a Brahmin priest, we suddenly find Him, at the age of twenty-nine, leaving His father's palace to become an ascetic living in the wilderness upon the charity of a strange community in order to solve the riddle of existence. Six years of the most persevering efforts and frightful privations leave Him physically exhausted, convinced that such a mode of life brings Him no nearer the solution of His problem—the world's problem—than did the life of splendour to which He had been accustomed. Finally, after deep meditation, sitting under the bo-tree, He discovers the secret of the Middle Path and all that pertains thereunto, obtains enlightenment, attains Nibbana, and has reached the end of His quest. And now, to acquaint mankind with His discovery, He taught incessantly, going from place to place, from His 36th to His 80th year, when He expired.

Thus it is not the land He inhabited that accounts for the nature of His teachings and their influence upon mankind as a whole, wonderful though that land was in His day ; nor was it the race to which He belonged, however high its intelligence; nor the climate in which He lived, however much it may have favoured or hampered the developmont of its inhabitants ; nor his early education, in which religion played but a minor part; nor, for that matter, the incidents in His life which, though somewhat unusual, were after all not so much out of the ordinary in a land where ascetics and yogis were the rule rather than the exception.

It is His teaching *per se* which commends itself to thinkers as the most illuminating reasoning over propounded, as the most humane doctrine ever preached, as the most complete and satisfactory solution to the riddle of existence, productive of the greatest and most permanent happiness to those who follow its simple precepts.

Whatever origin our speculators may assign to the Dhamma, the Buddha Himself claims to have been self-taught: He acknowledges no master, human or divine. Hence no effort has ever been made to represent Buddhism as a religion of revelation. It was the first missionary religion, and counted for obtaining adherents solely upon its inherent reasonableness. Herein not only lies the secret of its success, but also that of its persistence wherever may be found fearless and independent thinkers.

The keystone of the Buddhist arch is Wisdom: its sides are, on the one hand Compassion, on the other Reason. And through this arch, and this arch only, can we enter the realm of perfect balance, of unaffected bliss, of unchangeable selflessness—Nibbana!

THE GREAT RECOGNITIONS

The First Recognition: Unlike any other religion, Buddhism does not begin with any reference to a Creator or with any history of creation. Not that it ignores the God idea, as has been so frequently imputed to it: we shall find that dealt with in its proper place. But its first appeal to man is a call to look about himself. "Can you discover any phenomenon of existence that is not associated with suffering of some kind, either in the retrospect, the actual present, or the prospect?" And the longer you look, the less becomes the likelihood; the more thoroughly you investigate, the more deeply grows the conviction that, in truth, existence and suffering cannot be dissociated.

At first blush such a statement seems exaggerated. Shocking though it be to the imagination, it is not difficult to prove its correctness. Let us investigate.

All of us know what suffering is. Physical suffering is pain, such as a tooth-ache; emotional suffering is sorrow, such as we experience at the death of a wife, a mother, a friend; moral suffering is shame, such as we feel when we have betrayed the trust of a fellow being; mental suffering is worry or fear, such as we permit when we remember past suffering or are in the throes of present difficulties and cannot see relief ahead. Then there is the suffering of sympathy.

Now it is quite true that neither physical pain, nor sorrow, nor shame, nor worry or fear, are continuous. They are interspersed with periods not only of relief, but of actual joy. But that is merely due to the fact that for the time being our imagination is not working along the lines of either the past or the future. If we but stop to think for a moment it is immediately apparent that, just as past sufferings have been numerous and often unexpected, so the same will hold good for future woe in store for us. No pleasure is lasting, no joy remains; so that, in addition to the positive suffering of the evil to come, we have the negative pain of the cessation of the pleasurable condition.

But now suppose that we are unselfish enough to be able to forget our own distress; suppose that we insist mentally upon ignoring as much as possible our pains and our troubles. Even then we are never without relatives, friends, and acquaintances with whom we suffer sympathetically. It is simply impossible for us so to shut ourselves off from the world that we have not reason to sympathize.

So far we have considered only ourselves and our immediate circle. We should realize, however, that these few individuals form but the minutest portion of humanity at large. Most of us have imagination enough to realize that of the fifteen hundred million human beings on earth the majority at any given moment are in a condition of physical, emotional, moral or mental distress. All human beings are our brothers and our sisters. Creed or colour, class or race, we are all largely built upon the same mould; our appearance, our sensations, our perceptions, our tendencies, our consciousness, are mainly the same. Can we be so forgetful of our fellow-men that we could see them suffer without extending a helping hand? If not, neither can we mentally see them in agony without at least being touched by the sight. And to the imaginative mind this sight is constant.

How many new millions amongst mankind are stricken each day by sickness? How many die in torture of mind and body? How many each day are left bereft of their near ones and dear ones, not knowing what the next day may bring? How many are being maimed and disfigured?

We hear harrowing tales of starving nations, starving not on account of war, but in the midst of the very peace that preceded the recent world conflict. Famines in China often carry away millions of the population of the affected districts in one season. We need only refer to recent famines in Russia. In India one hundred million men, women and children go hungry from year's end to year's end with a hunger of which we have no conception; living on one meal every two or three days! "If we can eat food once in two days, we will not ask for more," says an inhabitant of that poverty-stricken country, expressing the modest demand of numberless of his compatriots: but even this poorest of comforts is denied them!

Such is the normal state of the human race at large. Nor have we touched upon the additional horrors of wars, simply because we may regard them as temporary and abnormal conditions.

Let us extend our view a trifle, and survey some of the workings in the animal kingdom, for the animals also are our brothers. For this purpose I cannot do better, I believe, than quote a few lines from that magnificent work on Buddhism by Sir Edwin Arnold, *The Light of Asia*, describing the wonderful peace overlying the landscape as the King Suddhodana, accompanied by his son Siddhártha who was to become the Buddha, went forth to see the beauty of spring when

. . . all the jungle laughed with nesting songs,
And all the thickets rustled with small life
Of lizard, bee, beetle, and creeping things
Pleased at the spring-time . . .
The blue doves cooed from every well, far off

The village drums beat for some marriage feast;
All things spoke peace and plenty, and the Prince
Saw and rejoiced. But looking deep, he saw
The thorns which grow upon this rose of life:
How the swart peasant sweated for his wage,
Toiling for leave to live; and how he urged
The great-eyed oxen through the flaming hours,
Goading their velvet flanks; then marked he, too,
How lizard fed on ant, and snake on him,
And kite on both; and how the fish-hawk robbed
The fish-tiger of that which it had seized;
The shrike chasing the bulbul, which did hunt
The jewelled butterflies; till everywhere
Each slew a slayer and in turn was slain,
Life living upon death. So the fair show
Veiled one vast, savage, grim conspiracy
Of mutual murder, from the worm to man,
Who himself kills his fellow; seeing which—
The hungry ploughman and his labouring kine,
Their dewlaps blistered with the bitter yoke,
The rage to live which makes all living strife—
The Prince Siddhártha sighed. "Is this," he said,
"That happy earth they brought me forth to see?
How salt with sweat the peasant's bread! how hard

The oxen's service! in the brake how fierce
The war of weak and strong! i' th' air what plots!
No refuge e'en in water . . ."

As if this condition of things were not bad enough, man has taken it upon himself materially to add to this "grim conspiracy of mutual murder" by killing millions upon millions of highly evolved and sensitive animals yearly under the pretext that he needs their flesh for his food. He does this in a cold-blooded and organized way. Entire countries on the surface of this globe are given over to the raising of cattle and sheep for the shambles, and the cruelties committed upon these dumb creatures to make their flesh more palatable; the horrible conditions under which they are transported to the slaughter houses and under which they are killed, leave one with a cold perspiration.

And then the millions of birds killed or half killed for the sake of their feathers, to tickle woman's vanity!

Nor must we forget to mention the indescribable cruelties committed in the name of science upon some of the most nearly human animals: vivisection, another deliberate addition to the aggregate of the world's pain, perpetrated with the intent to diminish suffering! We are not here considering the value of vivisection to the human race as conceived by our misguided scientific friends, merely pointing to the suffering deliberately added by misconceived human ingenuity to that already existing as a natural condition.

The very thought of this multitude of suffering ones sends a shudder of horror through our frame, brings a cry of despair to our lips. We are beginning to realize that human and animal existence, at least, is associated with pain both natural and artificially inflicted.

Looking upon the matter in another light, every creature that exists lives by virtue of the will to maintain itself, be it at the cost of other creatures. An inherent energy in each being endeavours to overcome the natural forces against which it is maintaining itself. As long as it thus maintains itself satisfactorily it feels little discomfort, though the effort may be very strenuous; but if at any time the opposing forces are not sufficiently held at bay, disease sets in, with decrepitude and death in its wake, all accompanied by friction, distress and pain.

The first great concept set forth by the Buddha is the noble recognition of suffering: "This, O Monks, is the Noble Truth concerning Suffering: birth is suffering, decrepitude is suffering, sickness is suffering, death is suffering; to be bound to the unloved is suffering, to be separated from the loved is suffering, not to obtain one's desires is suffering; in short, the fivefold clinging to existence is suffering!"

No doubt we shall be told that such a view of existence is far too pessimistic to appeal to mankind in general. This objection has been frequently made against the Buddhistic view of things, but its shallowness is easily demonstrated. In reality Buddhism points out a sure way to deliverance from suffering, and is therefore truly optimistic in purpose and effect. For how could we eliminate suffering unless we recognized it first? To recognize it to its fullest extent, in all its bearings; to look our enemy in the face unflinchingly, courageously; this constitutes the first step towards his undoing. As long as we run, the dogs of suffering are at our heels; but let us make a stand and face them, and they will slink off one after the other until they are all gone, and we are free from both fear and the pursuit of the dogs!

Thus it is that the first appeal on the part of Buddhism is to open our mental eyes, that they may see things as they really are, that they may recognize the friction involved in the very act of living, that they may understand that existence cannot be dissociated from suffering. If once the truth of this statement has come home to us, if it has penetrated to the very depth of our consciousness in all its unpleasant reality, we can proceed to take the next step along the path of recognition and inquire as to the cause of this condition of things.

The Second Recognition: We have seen that there is no life without friction, no existence without suffering, not resulting in suffering, or not conducive to suffering physical, mental, emotional, or sympathetic. What then is the origin of this suffering, what its cause?

Once more we are called upon to look within ourselves. No arbitrary statements are made in Buddhistic reasoning. If but we have a clear perception of the processes with which our life is bound up, which constitute our existence, we can almost divine the anwer. It is thirst, craving, that is the cause of all suffering: thirst for pleasure, for prosperity, for power, for things we have not, things we want, things we see others have!

Better to understand this apparently simple solution we will have to investigate some of the forces governing existence in this world from a perhaps somewhat unusual angle.

According to the Buddhistic conception, life is not limited to three score years and ten. This present span is but an incident in a continuous and virtually endless process. Modern theories of evolution have paved the way for the acceptance of such a view in the western world. We are given to understand that from the mineral kingdom to man there may be assumed an unbroken chain of forms, one leading to the next, until we reach the human. True, there are many side branches, and many of the links between one form and the next have disappeared. But the main line is clearly discernible. Upon this discovery is based the theory of evolution which assumes that, since this line exists, man must have climbed it from the very lowest shape to the form with which he is endowed at the present time.

But the evolutionary theory has never been able to account for the impulse which caused this climbing process to go on. What was it that made the mineral gradually lift itself to the level of the vegetable? What caused the plant to acquire animal characteristics? And what, finally, was the impulse driving the animal to the human stage?

Here we enter a delicate field of speculation. Theology answers the question simply by saying "God"; Science speaks of an "inherent trend"; Philosophy points out that either of these answers leaves us exactly where we were at the propounding of the question, for though both of them may be true, neither of them is explanatory!

From the Buddhist point of view we regard all that exists not as merely endowed with life, but as living. The dust mote in the sunbeam, the sunbeam itself, the sun, the earth, men, animals, plants, minerals, all that *is*, *lives*: existence is life, being is living.

Let us not confuse this thought with the pantheistic statement that universal life *pervades* all things. The latter view postulates life as a separate something and then proceeds to permeate all things with it. The Buddhist, on the other hand, regards life as the very being of the existing thing. To the extent that it *is*, to that extent is it life: the material of which the thing is composed is not something through which life works or manifests, but is that very life itself. Matter and Life can *never* be dissociated.

Now there are all grades of materiality. Matter does not end with the solid, the liquid and the gaseous, or even with the etheric substances. True, our senses do not respond to any finer grades of matter, but that is simply due to the fact that they themselves are mainly composed of the grosser kinds. To senses themselves made up of finer material such matter would be quite as objective as our present material is to the senses with which physically we are endowed.

But Buddhism does not permit us to accuse it of being materialistic, in spite of the fact that it sees nothing but matter wherever it looks. For matter to it means something more than what usually goes by that name. The Buddhistic view does not countenance an ultimate atomic substance. When we get to the atom of one kind of substance, we have to deal with a new complex of the next grade; bring this again down to *its* atoms, and we have a complex of the next grade of matter; and so on, indefinitely. But all these complexities of structure are complexities of life as well—not just endowed with life—on the principle that life and matter cannot ever be dissociated, and they are complexities of life to the same extent that they are complexities of structure and material.

To the Buddhist there is nothing ever dead; there are only different kinds of life. When a man dies, his body immediately begins to live another kind of existence. Released from what held it together as an organized unit, each cell or group of cells continues to live separately and thus decay sets in. That which controlled the body is still in existence though it has given up control over the outworn physical vehicle. It is still in material existence, but of a material to which our physical senses do not respond. Therefore we do not see it, or hear it, or feel it, unless our finer senses are awakened and we are aware of it by their means. But both the body and that which controlled the body continue to live; for nothing dies: only the *kind* of life changes.

Two great divisions of life are recognized: that life which forms an organized unit, an I; and that which does not. Wherein lies the difference?

The life which forms a separate unit, an I, may be compared to a knot or a complex of knots on a string. It is the same string and yet each knot constitutes a separate entity. The string has not changed, except in appearance. The knot is only the string wound about itself, yet not separated from the remainder of the string.

Now if we imagine portions of the string gradually tying themselves into more and more complicated knots, reacting upon local impulses, we have the Buddhist conception of evolution. For each knot that ties itself, we have a greater strain upon the remainder of the cord ; and the more it winds itself, and the larger it grows, the greater strength must it exert to hold itself together, to maintain its individuality against the pull which itself has created.

With the aid of this simile we can perhaps better understand why individual existence is struggle, is friction, is suffering. The strain to maintain individuality is constant, and always at the expense of the whole ; more especially, however, at the expense of those particular individuals with which the original self comes into direct contact. Whenever, therefore, such a self becomes still more insistent, still more complex, the strain and the struggle correspondingly increase !

What is it in the first instance that causes the consciousness of self, of individuality ? Let us once more revert to our simile. The moment a portion of the string gets twisted around once so as to form a loop, that moment a self has come into being. As soon as there is a circumference, there is a centre, there is a reflection, there is self-recognition, there is self-consciousness, there is a here and a there, space and contact, sensation and desire, memory and a tendency to persist as a separate self, with its consequent strain and suffering.

Individual existence once having been attained, the taste for it grows with each sip. The desires become more complex and more difficult to satisfy; and the oftener they are satisfied, the more complex they become. It is like drinking sea water to quench one's thirst: the more one drinks, the greater becomes the thirst.

That is why thirst, craving, is the cause of all suffering. The impulse behind evolution is both "God" and "inherent". It is "God" in the sense that we are but cells within the body of a more complex being, who in his turn is a cell in the body of a being holding the same relation to him as he does to us. So the cells of which our body is composed combine to form our complexity, but they in their turn are immense beings to the cells which constitute *them*. We may repeat these processes in corresponding magnitudes indefinitely in either direction: each complexity is as "God" to its cells; each "God" a cell in the next higher complex; each cell a God to *its* constituent units . . . The impulse in question is "inherent" because it is the force of desire which causes it to reach out further and further, to assert itself more and more, to enter upon the grind of life and death, of birth and rebirth; first as one form, then as another; ever more complex, ever evolving; until at last the human stage is reached with its more intense selfness, its greater means for self-gratification, its subtler cravings, its deeper and more sympathetic suffering.

Let us understand therefore what is the origin of suffering, the second great recognition. Says the Buddha: "This, O Monks, is the Noble Truth concerning the Origin of Suffering: thirst for life, which leads from birth to birth, together with lust and desire, which finds gratification here and there; the thirst for pleasure, the thirst for existence, the thirst for power."

The Third Recognition: Thus far we have found that there is suffering, that it is inextricably bound up with existence, and that thirst, or craving, is the cause of this suffering. Let us see what we must next recognize.

Whenever we concede the presence of an undesirable condition and understand its cause, the logical step towards abolishing such a condition is to abolish this cause. That is, of course, more easily said than done. If I am hungry and want something to eat, I know that by getting something to eat my hunger will be appeased. But to know that that is the case, and to *find* the food that will suitably appease my hunger, are two different things.

Now we know that there is suffering, and we know that craving is the cause of suffering. We next must set ourselves suitably to abolish this craving for existence, for change, for pleasure, for power, for self-gratification!

Just as we have seen that there are different kinds of suffering—physical, moral, emotional, mental—so we have also different kinds of craving which may be similarly classified and which ultimately give rise to their respective counterparts of suffering. For example, the craving for physical pleasures, such as worldly comfort or luxury, will have the effect of directing our energies toward their acquisition. As long as our craving remains unsatisfied we are working and scheming, hoping and fearing, restless and longing: never happy. Now we may either succeed in getting what we have craved for; not succeed in getting it; or else lose our desire for the thing craved before having acquired it.

1. If we do succeed in getting what we are craving, either we will want more of it and keep on craving; or we now set to craving something else; or we are temporarily satisfied. In the last case our satisfaction hardly can very long endure because we have accustomed ourselves to the life of the hunter and have acquired, with the thing we sought, a hunting disposition which must be eradicated before contentment can be found. Now the thing achieved will either prove

disappointing, or else it will satisfy. If it is disappointing, there is disgust. If it satisfies, there must come a time when it has to be given up again, when its loss becomes a new source of regret.

2. If we do not succeed in achieving the things craved for, we will either despair, or else become still more discontented and envious of others who did get what we failed to obtain.

3. Should we lose the desire for the thing before having acquired it, and cease to work for its acquisition, we have yet set in motion forces which will tend to bring the thing in question ultimately, even though it be no longer desired, in fact, when it has become distinctly undesirable from the point of view changed by the lapse of time.

The very act of craving has the same effect upon human existence as the act of winding has upon a clock: it increases the driving force and prolongs the go—not so much the physical go as the entire combination of physical existences together with their intervening periods. Craving is the force that drives us from birth to birth, from life to life, wearying us with fresh weariness, increasing our sensibilities, making us susceptible to greater suffering: in fine, it is the cause of evolution. How difficult to stop the swiftly spinning wheel; how small the force required to keep it spinning!

*2

I said that if we cease to work for something we at one time craved, it may yet be brought about ultimately. This statement bears a little qualifying.

The energy generated by the act of craving is directive. That is to say, whenever we crave, we crave for *something,* and the energy so generated will tend to bring that something about. How? First of all by making us work for it, consciously or unconsciously; secondly, by bringing us into touch with it, directly or indirectly; thirdly, by making us acquire it or become identified with it. Now the longer a craving is sustained, the more energy is generated, and the more easily the thing craved for is acquired. But if half along the road towards acquisition my energy begins to flag, my desire wanes, my craving for that particular thing weakens, it is obvious that I cannot attain the end in view. But it is also clear that the energy I have already spent is not lost. Something has been set in motion. It may be compared to throwing a ball. If I change my mind in the midst of the act of throwing I may not be able to stay my hand altogether. The ball will leave with but part of the energy I had meant to put into the throw and, though not reaching its goal, will yet roll in the latter's general direction.

Now this is just what happens when we long for something without having first decided that it is the thing to long for. The force with which we crave generates a certain amount of energy. That energy tends in the general direction of the thing craved. If enough of that energy is released the thing craved for will be acquired or achieved. If not, it may be partially acquired ; at any rate, the tendency towards its acquisition will have become established.

The tragedy of wanting a thing without due consideration—let us say that one of our most sincere longings when a child, was to become a railway conductor—is that our whole mentality will acquire a general bent toward the thing in question, and should we see the error of our way—let us say that we finally come to the conclusion that, after all, to become a railway conductor is not our avocation—we not merely have to correct our mental leaning, but give it a new direction into the bargain. Moreover, whatever energy has been released has taken wing along the former line of longing and cannot now be re-called : it will, therefore, cause us to lean somewhat in the railway conductor direction until it has exhausted itself.

This principle, by the way, is the one underlying New Thought, Christian Science, and similar movements. They all tell us that whatever we desire strongly enough and definitely enough we shall obtain, be it health, wealth, or power. But they forget to tell us one thing, the very thing upon which Buddhism lays more stress even than upon this natural law, namely that, whatever we acquire we must also lose again as soon as the force behind the acquisition, the force of the original craving, has spent itself. It is then that we suffer doubly, for it is harder to miss what we have become accustomed to, than not to get what we do not expect.

And then there is still another factor that we must consider. The cravings of our previous existences predispose us to our present cravings. If they have been specific along certain lines—say the desire to become a builder of houses—the results will also be specific as far as the new circumstances will allow. In the next birth, then, we shall become builders of dwellings through an innate tendency that will drive us in that direction. In our childhood we shall show aptitude in building with nursery blocks: in youth we shall desire to erect tents and shelters, or study architecture; in manhood we shall become building contractors or architects. Since there is always an intermingling accumulation of energies from previous cravings, some stronger, some weaker, some more definite, some less so, they will all of them tend to come to the surface sooner or later, as opportunities present themselves and as they are evoked by circumstance. That is why human life is so varied and in many respects so contradictory. Whatever energy has been generated, that must also be released. Craving generates energy: action releases it. Hundreds of cravings have given us an accumulation of energy: we are therefore capable of hundreds of different kinds of actions. But the most dominant cravings find vent in the most distinct activities.

From this we may readily gather that whatever happens to us, is coming to us, is deserved. Good, bad, or indifferent, it has been our own making, our own kamma. No one else is to blame, no God and no Devil. We should accept, therefore, whatever comes of evil with resignation; whatever of good without elation.

This tendency to action, this generated and stored-up energy is what constitutes our self. We are nothing more nor less than *tendency to action*, resulting from craving. This is our self, our I, our individuality, our character. It is our capacity to respond. Even as a gong, when struck, will resound with its own particular tone and volume, depending upon the kind of metal of which it is composed, the shape it holds, the way it is suspended, and the strength of the blow; so each of us, when being acted upon by our environment, will respond in a particular fashion. And the tendency to respond thus and not otherwise is our self, our individuality, our kamma, as the Buddhist calls it. Not that we *have* this particular kind of responsiveness, but we *are* it. *That* we are, and nothing more. And just as little as the particular sound of the gong can be called the soul of the gong, so our character, our tendencies, our individuality, cannot properly be called our soul, in the sense that the word is in usage.

Thus it is said very often that the Buddhist does not believe in a soul! But that is only partly true, as we shall see later when dealing specifically with this subject. What we may state here is that what is usually called a "soul," the Buddhist regards as the capacity to respond to external impact upon the senses, upon the feelings, upon the mind. This is our kamma, our action, our self, our soul, if you wish. And by craving we add to this kamma. Only by ceasing to crave can we permit our present kamma to exhaust itself. Only by cultivating contentment under any and all circumstances can we abandon desire. Only by ceasing to cling with our senses, our feelings and our thought to the objects of sense can we eliminate desire for them.

Craving is like adding fuel to a fire. As long as we are dominated by desire, as long as the fever of craving rages, so long the fire of suffering must burn. As soon as we recognize that we ourselves are the originators of our own distress, are wholly to blame for the pain with which we are afflicted at any time, even though it seems to come through others (for we must remember that many times in the age-long past we did cause others suffering which returns to us similarly), we shall also see the wisdom of cultivating perfect acquiescence in whatever befalls us. For through such acquiescence only can the fire of craving be gradually extinguished. It is our recognition that we are paying for what we have had, that we are willing to pay, that we do not endeavour to evade payment. It is also our recognition that it is wiser to contract no further debts, for no other reason than that debts imply the necessity of having to pay them, the impossibility of ultimately evading payment: all of which cannot be accomplished without suffering.

Buddhism, as its name implies, is the religion of wisdom. We must avoid things because it is wise to avoid them, not because some one, be it God or Man, tells us that they ought to be avoided. The Buddhist avoids those things which ultimately bring pain. To him only that is evil which brings pain sooner or later. He hurts no creature, animal or man. Wherever he goes he brings kindliness. He is enjoined by the Buddha to love all creatures "as a mother loves her child, her only child" He makes no distinction between good men and bad men. If anything, he loves the bad man more. For, says the Buddha, "who would willingly use harsh speech to those who have done a sinful deed, strewing salt, as it were, upon the wound of their fault?" If a man commits a hurtful deed, he will surely reap the result of that deed. Then why should we add to the suffering which he has prepared for himself by condemning him or by punishing him? By giving way to our desire to retaliate we only perpetuate and enlarge the evil already done. Let us avoid the things that hurt us. Whatever hurts us is deserved by us, has been brought about by us, even though it come through others. Whatever may hurt others must be avoided, may not be done. Only thus can we end kamma, cease reacting, cultivate contentment, contract no new debts, lessen suffering. For whatever suffering may be left in the world, that which would have been our contribution to it will have been withdrawn and will not circulate. And in return, no suffering of which we have not been the author can lay hold on us, for we give it nothing to lay hold of.

Our third recognition therefore is the realization that, since craving is the source of all suffering, of all evolution, of all action and reaction; since it perpetuates conditions which themselves invariably give rise to further suffering: since it winds the clock of existence in the general direction of the craving indulged: we must do away with this craving, this futile longing, this unholy, self-increasing thirst. In the words of the Buddha: "This, O Monks, is the Noble Truth concerning the Cessation of Suffering: the cessation of this thirst by the complete absence of craving, abandoning it, expelling it, separating from it, giving it no hold."

And the Way which cannot fail to lead to the extinction of this thirst is the Noble Eightfold Path, which constitutes the Fourth Great Recognition.

THE NOBLE EIGHTFOLD PATH

SAYS the Buddha : " This, O Monks, is the Noble Truth of the Path which leads to the Cessation of Suffering, The Noble Eightfold Path, namely :

I. Right Understanding
Right Mindedness

II. Right Speech
Right Action
Right Livelihood

III. Right Endeavour
Right Recollectedness
Right Rapture."

The Path may be divided into three sections. The first of these consists of two, the second and third each of three divisions. The whole practical effect of Buddhist teaching is summed up in the Noble Eightfold Path and it is therefore essential that we deal with it somewhat at length.

The first section of the Path comprises Right Understanding and Right Mindedness ; that is to say, after we have understood the purport of the teaching we must make up our minds to live it. This section, therefore, is the preliminary one, the one in which we have become convinced of the correctness of the Buddha's teaching, of its practicability and of its desirability, whereupon we decide to live in accordance with this understanding. For it is as unwise to understand it without living it, as it is inconsistent to try to live the teaching without understanding its purport.

The Buddha does not ask us to act in mere faith. We are enjoined before all things to understand. Buddhism is not a religion of faith in any sense of the word: it is a religion of understanding, of compassion, of wisdom. And if the morality which is the outcome of our own understanding is at least as sublime as that based on faith in other religions, it would seem as if the former would be the more stable of the two. For faith is blind, whilst understanding is mental vision. Moral action based on understanding is truly intuitive, whereas that based upon prescription, upon faith, has to be learnt by rote and is mechanical. The man with understanding can act spontaneously and rightly under all conditions; the man who has nothing but faith to guide him will act in the *hope* that he may have acted rightly under the circumstances.

Understanding, therefore, is the first requisite in Buddhism and is placed first in the Noble Eightfold Path. To decide to live in accordance with correct understanding is the next requirement.

These two represent the preparatory section of the Path that produces wisdom and insight.

The next section comprises three divisions, namely Right Speech, Right Action, Right Livelihood, thus constituting the ethical aspect of the Path. To know what to say and how to say it; truth, no falsehood; no evil, no slander; not to speak angrily or abusively, but courteously and kindly; not pointless and foolish talks, but speech sensible and to the purpose: that is Right Speech. We must act uprightly and harmlessly. We must earn our livelihood honestly and hurtlessly. These are three requirements strictly insisted upon by Buddhism, fully grasped by all whose faculties of understanding have become awakened by the Buddha's teachings.

The third section of the Noble Eightfold Path represents the mental aspect of the system. It teaches us what kind of endeavour should be made; to remember the lessons taught by such endeavour; and its resultant attitude with the rapture attendant upon it. As a man carrying a heavy burden will endeavour to rid himself of the weight he is sustaining, and by the proper kind of recollectedness discovers a way to do so, and having done so will heave a sigh of relief; so the man travelling the Noble Eightfold Path endeavours to rid himself of the burden of suffering, and by the proper kind of recollectedness succeeds in finding a method of doing so, and having done so will experience a state of rapture akin to that of a freed galley slave.

It must be explained that the Noble Eightfold Path is not a path in the ordinary sense of the word. We cannot take the eight steps one by one. It is impossible, for example, to attain full measure of Right Understanding without attaining in some measure any of the other steps, just as it is impossible to learn to operate any kind of machinery, say a typewriter, by merely studying how it should be done. Theoretical understanding is never complete understanding. You may study the keyboard of a typewriter until you know it by heart, and the mechanism of its action until there is not a part with which you are not acquainted, yet when set before an actual typewriter and requested to operate it you cannot do so with the ease, grace and rapidity of even the average typist with far less theoretical knowledge. Unless theory and practice go together all the factors involved do not come into play. The proper way to learn to operate any machine is to study its principles and to learn to handle it at the same time, and as the understanding of the way in which the machine works improves so also increases the facility of handling it.

The same holds good for the Noble Eightfold Path. As we obtain Right Understanding, so we exercise Right Mindedness ; so will we control our speech and direct our actions and earn our livelihood in a proper manner ; so also will we make the Right Endeavour, practise Right Recollectedness and experience the consequent Rapture ; all of which will again improve our understanding of things, which in turn will stimulate our right mindedness, affect our speech, our conduct, our means of earning a livelihood, increase our right endeavour, our recollectedness and our rapture ; and so again improve our understanding, and so on. It acts in a circle, a virtuous circle, not a vicious one this time.

This is indicated by the use of the word "sammā" in the original Pali, somewhat inadequately translated by the word "right" in English. We have no one word properly to express the meaning of "sammā" in this connection. Right Understanding is more correctly rendered by "understanding after having surveyed the whole field". So Right Mindedness by "that mental decision consequent upon the survey of the field of understanding". Right Speech, again, would be more correctly rendered by "that speech which is found to be proper after having duly considered all circumstances," and so on. The word "sammā" can best be understood when we say it of a man who, having reached the top of a mountain, in looking about himself has a "sammā" view of the surrounding country. To say that he has the right view is almost saying the same thing, though not quite: he has the adequate view. The man who has the "sammā" view, the summit view, is certainly more likely to have the right view, the better proportioned view, than the one who is looking around below in the valley. It is therefore necessary for the proper understanding of the meaning of the Noble Eightfold Path to qualify the word "Right" which precedes each of its stages, in accordance with this explanation.

Now let us examine each individual stage of the Noble Eightfold Path, realizing that they are all more or less co-progressive, that they must be cultivated more or less together, that it avails us little to understand its mechanism without at the same time putting our hand to the machinery.

The Preliminary Steps: It is obvious that by Right Understanding, the first stage of the Path, is meant such understanding as is engendered by a survey of the whole field of Buddhist teaching. This is not a matter that can be disposed of in a few words; in fact, these studies in Buddhism collectively are but an attempt in that direction, and may therefore be regarded as an aid to such a survey. Preliminarily, however, a right understanding of the Four Noble Truths: the existence of suffering, its nature and cause, the possibility of its removal, and the path to its cessation; is necessary. It must also be understood that the value of knowledge of any kind is to be tested on the touchstone of its capacity to remove suffering. If capable of diminishing suffering such knowledge is of value ; if it does not tend to diminish suffering, it is useless ; if it increases suffering, even temporarily, it is false knowledge. The Buddhist believes that, though a little knowledge be a dangerous thing, no knowledge at all is the cause of all evil. He calls this ignorance, Avijjā, and when he enumerates the causes productive of suffering, it heads the list as the first link in a twelve sectioned chain.

False knowledge or delusion is that kind of knowledge which gives rise to new or perpetuates existing suffering. It is this sort of pseudo-knowledge with which our scientists are engaged when they endeavour to eliminate disease by inflicting the worst imaginable torture upon living creatures by means of vivisection on the plea that the end justifies the means. It is also that kind of knowledge which has for its purpose the satisfaction of our desires or their stimulation, such as that connected with the acquisition of wealth, the preparation of dainty food, the manufacture of intoxicating drink, elaborate and over-stylish dress, the indulgence in unnecessary and luxurious comfort, the ruling over and exacting obedience from other men, and so on.

It is so much more difficult to unlearn than to learn ! When we have no knowledge at all on any particular subject it is not hard to acquire some. But if we have false knowledge on any point and do not recognize it as false, it is the greatest obstacle in the path to progress. It requires a a peculiar openness of mind and a willingness to consider all views, to overcome the prejudice engendered by false knowledge. For it is not recognized as prejudice by its unfortunate possessors who continue blindly to pursue their subject until finally, perhaps after many lives and extreme suffering, they are willing to let go and search for the truth in another direction.

Kamma, the law of reaction, of the interconnection of events, as summed up in the Buddha's words : "That being present, this becomes ; from the arising of that, this arises ; that being absent, this does not become ; from the cessation of that, this ceases," must be thoroughly comprehended. And the right understanding of this principle, simple as a child's thought, yet deep as reaches the mind of man, is a prime necessity.

That all Life is but a becoming, that nothing is the same for two consecutive moments of time, that all things and conditions are changeable and passing, that nothing is stable even for an instant ; these things must be understood before the Path can be trodden to advantage.

The question of the nature of Time must be understood. To the Buddhist view a second may be as prolonged as a day or a year, as a century or a millennium, according to the sense of the being appreciating it. On the other hand, a millennium, a century, a year, a day, may be as short as a second by the same token. Whether certain joys lasted an æon, a lifetime, or but a moment, it matters not: they are past and that proves their ephemeral nature. All the millions of years of history have elapsed, and yet humanity is still steeped in the deepest and most pitiful ignorance. Was it ever different? The Buddhist emphatically answers "No!" It has always been so and it always will be more or less alike, not because there is no progression, but because there always is an influx from below as there is an efflux from above. The past has vanished, and so is the present constantly vanishing. The past is no more, the present is constantly changing, the future is ever ahead.

The follower of the Buddha lives in the present only. For him the past has no practical meaning; the future only in so far as it perpetuates the present. How to do away with the present, then, how to eliminate the sense of time, that must be understood rightly before the Path can be profitably trodden.

And with the elimination of the sense of time must go the elimination of the sense of self. As long as our self is insisted on in any way, shape or form, so long will time be felt, so long will change affect us, so long will suffering remain. When are we happiest? When we succeed in forgetting ourselves. When goes time quickest? When we forget ourselves. When can there be no pain? When we forget ourselves. In fact, the Buddhist goes so far as to say that time, self and suffering are synonymous! That must be understood rightly before the Path can be trodden to advantage.

That craving, grasping, cleaving, clinging, are the producers of suffering and the perpetuators of suffering, that must be rightly understood. Tanha, that thirst of the mind which goes after existence as the thirst of the throat goes after drink, that craving after sensation, must be gradually eliminated by cultivating an attitude of contentment with whatever befalls. For whatever befalls has been of our own making. The lesson to be learnt is not how to evade it: that can be done at best temporarily only; but how not to produce the same effect again, that is the chief object in view when we are dissatisfied with events. For it is by attachment, by clinging, by grasping, by craving that we suffer and never cease to suffer until it occurs to us that the things we cling to are but temporary, the things we crave worthless. That must be understood rightly before the Path can become productive of benefit.

It is not necessary to understand these and other fundamentals all at once; that is a gradual process. But it is wise for us to inquire into them and to build our mental attitude upon them, to speak and act and live in accord with them, to aim at and to remember them, and experience a stimulating joy as they gradually penetrate and and permeate our consciousness. Right Understanding is the aim as well as the end of the Noble Eightfold Path. Once acqired, it perpetuates itself and will underlie our very being as the keynote to our capacity to react, and to the nature of our reaction.

And then, when dealing with Right Mindedness, we may think of it as the resolution to put into practice such understanding as we may gradually acquire. At first we will experience considerable misgiving towards making such a resolve. Our entire environment requires a compromise between what we understand and what of it we can conveniently put into practice. We are constantly impelled to act against our better knowledge. But we are not compelled to do so. We should sit down and have a heart to heart talk with ourselves whenever we understand a thing one way and are urged to act in contravention. And the ultimate outcome of such a method indicates what we are minded to do. It is a check on our Right Mindedness. To the extent that we do not fall short of a decision to act in accordance with our understanding, to that extent are we mastering the second step upon the Noble Eightfold Path.

The resolution to mould our speech, our action, our livelihood upon our own understanding of things, however faulty that understanding as yet may be, is the only resolution Buddhism requires of its votaries. If our understanding falls short, due to ignorance or false knowledge, we shall certainly draw upon ourselves the consequences of our acts and learn to correct our understanding by the suffering thus engendered. But, having Himself acquired through æons of personal experience, unsurpassed insight, the Buddha places at our disposal His supreme wisdom as a guide and a stimulant to our understanding. He lays down no dogma. His expressed wish is that we do not accept even His version of things simply on the strength of His say-so. But if we so desire we may turn to and consider and profit by His experience and insight, and thus save ourselves the lengthy process of gradually finding out things through painful reactions. He has discovered the Law governing suffering, and places His discovery at our disposal. It is, without exception, the greatest and most vital discovery ever made!

But He does not lay down the law: He merely calls attention to it. He does not ask of us to act in accordance with *His* understanding, but rather to correct our own and then act in accordance with ours. We are reminded that behaviour based upon our own insight is the only method by which to correct that insight. Consequently it is of the utmost importance that we resolve to put our understanding to the test of practical experience, and it is that resolution which constitutes Right Mindedness.

The Ethical Triplicity: Having thus resolved, the next step along the Middle Path is not action, as we might have thought, but Right Speech. It is a very significant thing that of the three divisions, Right Speech, Right Action, and Right Livelihood, comprising the practical or ethical section of the Noble Eightfold Path, speech should be placed first. A little thought will show how rational and human a touch of wisdom this is. The Path is nothing if not practical, and it is human nature to precede deliberate action by verbal consideration. Whether this refers to speech with others or with ourselves, aloud, in whispers, or in thought, makes no difference. Before we act we must think, talk things over with ourselves or with others, and it is only after due deliberation that we should proceed.

Right speech is exercised in four distinct ways :

(1) To speak only that which is true, not what is false ;

(2) To speak no evil of others and refrain from slander ;

(3) To use no angry and abusive language, but ever to speak kindly and courteously ;

(4) Not to indulge in pointless or foolish talk, but to speak sensibly and to the purpose.

Strange to say, the above rules hold good not only in the exercise of the faculty of speech as regards our fellow-men, but should be observed also in reference to our thinking faculty, our self-speech. We may not speak differently to ourselves from how we speak to others. Even our speech and behaviour to animals, be they domestic or untamed, is based upon the same principles of kindness and courtesy, of tenderness and consideration. When upon a certain occasion it was reported to the Buddha that one of His monks had been bitten by a poisonous snake and had died of his wound, the Buddha exclaimed that this was due to the fact that the monk in question had not had love in his heart towards snakes, for one with love in his heart towards snakes they would never hurt.

Right Action is closely allied to Right Speech—speech being a form of action—but it refers to deeds done by the body rather than to those committed verbally. The outstanding feature of the meaning of Right Action is harmlessness. To act in such a manner that no hurt is done to any living creature, oneself included, is the aim sought. Man is not by any manner of means the most important creature living, though he regards himself as such. There are beings as far beyond man in consciousness and intelligence as man is above the animal or plant, and further. The brotherhood of man does not begin to comprise the sense of brotherhood of the Buddhist. His feeling of brotherhood extends to all that lives, without exception.

Now it is quite true that in a world where the very continuation of human life depends upon the encroachment of man upon other kingdoms, the ideal of harmlessness cannot always be maintained. But it *is* feasible to reduce this quite inevitable infringement upon the potential well-being of other creatures to the narrowest possible limits. This can be achieved by exercising Right Action governed by the following four restrictions: (1) Refraining from inflicting wounds or death; (2) Refraining from taking things that have not been voluntarily given; (3) Refraining from the ungranted gratification of one's lust; (4) Refraining from the indulgence in intoxicating liquors and stupefying drugs.

The first of these four restrictions not merely refers to human beings, including oneself, but to animal life as well and in a measure even to vegetable existence, more specifically to the nobler creatures of the plant kingdom, the trees. No one who wishes to observe this injunction of the Enlightened One will make requirements involving the suffering or death of any human or animal being, be it for industrial reasons or for the nourishment or the adornment of the human body. Animal food is not necessary for the sustenance of life: in fact, it is detrimental to human well-being. Vegetable food is natural to man, but it must always be eaten in as nearly its native condition as possible. This does not mean that it should not be cooked or prepared, but that it ought not to be deprived of vital portions before it serves as food. Flour, for instance, should be whole, that is to say, every portion of the grain should be present; fruit, whenever possible, should be eaten with its skin; vegetables without having their salts extracted by faulty cooking.

Unless absolutely necessary, trees should not be injured or cut down.

The injunction not to inflict wounds or death is not a fanatical prescription, however. It is sufficient to exercise reasonable care in its observance. A story is related in one of the early Buddhist books of a monk who, having strained his drinking water in accordance with the Buddha's precept, still saw, by means of his spiritual vision, the water full of innumerable animalculæ. For that reason he hesitated to drink it, and going to the Buddha, he asked what he was to do under the circumstances. Whereupon the Buddha let it be known that, having used the water strainer, all reasonable requirements had been fulfilled. In this, as in all other matters, the Buddhist view avoids the falseness of extremes.

Supreme sanity is the constant characteristic of the Middle Path.

The second injunction is directed against stealing or, to be more accurate, against taking things that have not been voluntarily given, implying the full and free consent of the giver. Even trees are not to be deprived of their fruit until they voluntarily surrender it, that is to say, until it is actually ripe enough to fall off.

The wording of this injunction is such that there is no loophole for the acquisition of possessions by any questionable means that do not specifically fall under the head of stealing, as by deceit or under duress. Acting in accordance with this precept, honesty and uprightness of conduct are absolutely unavoidable in all dealings between all classes of men, in trivial affairs as in great matters. No room whatsoever is left for any dispute here, or equivocation.

The third injunction is directed against unlawful sex gratification. This has a somewhat different application to the layman from what it has to the bhikkhu or monk. In the case of the former there is no objection to sex indulgence within lawful limits which may vary according to custom, provided no being, living or to live, is wronged thereby. But for that follower of the Buddha who has cast off all worldly ties, who is permeated with His Teaching "as the cloth with the dye in the dyer's vat," all sex gratification is a hindrance and must be renounced, since it constitutes the culmination of the desire for existence, for the very contrary of which he has left the world.

The last of the four injunctions guiding Right Action exhorts us to refrain from indulging in intoxicating liquors and stupefying drugs. It is the earliest example we have in religious or social history of total prohibition! However, it is not fanaticism that prompts this regulation. Sane common sense tells us that a man when under the influence of liquor, however kind, self-restrained and honest he may be normally, is likely to break every precept of right conduct, quite independently of the damage done to the sensitiveness of his physical and nervous organism.

It is true that in a society living upon food that, by faulty methods of growing, marketing and preparation, has been deprived to a great extent of its mineral contents so necessary to the proper and balanced functioning of the body, the prohibition of the lighter alcohol-containing beverages such as wine, is worse than foolish, for the reason that these drinks contain in an organic and digestible form the very mineral substances the body requires and craves, whilst the alcohol acts as a counter-poison to the toxic animal substances introduced. But if once we revert to those more natural methods of nutrition prevalent before "science" taught us how to process our produce, and we cease to raise our crops with unbalanced fertilizers, the Buddhist precept of total prohibition can be followed with the utmost advantage to mankind.

Whenever we are under the influence of drink or drug the consciousness accompanying any act, whether good, bad, or indifferent, is less clear than it would be under normal conditions, with the result that its effect upon our faculty of understanding is less enlightening. And since all behaviour has but the one purpose namely to approximate Right Understanding, it is obvious that any act committed with a clouded consciousness fails to react upon our understanding to the extent that our awareness was beclouded.

For the Buddhist must be awake in order to derive the fullest possible measure of benefit from the teachings of the Awakened One. And whenever he gives himself over to conditions that produce violent reactions, in swinging from one to the other he damages his sensibilities, impairs his sensitiveness, and fails to attain and maintain that condition of sane balance requisite to the successful treading of the Middle Path.

The next factor to be considered is *Right Livelihood.* We must earn our livelihood honestly and hurtlessly, and not put ourselves in a position where we are compelled to violate these two requirements.

Specific directions are given in this case as in the cases of Right Action and Right Speech. We may not earn our living by the trade of killing our fellow-men, nor by any thing that contributes thereto, such as the manufacture or sale of lethal weapons which cause us to become accessories to the deed of killing. This means that the follower of the Buddha may not become a *professional* soldier. Nor may we manufacture poisons or deal in them, that is to say, of course, poisons intended to take human life, a not uncommon activity in the Orient.

The same directions hold good in regard to the taking of animal life, the manufacture or sale of implements used for that purpose, and the manufacture or sale of animal killing poisons. This precept, therefore, is designed to prevent us from becoming hunters, butchers, trappers, furriers, feather merchants, fishermen or dealers in such articles as pertain to these occupations.

Nor are we permitted to earn our livelihood by the capture and imprisonment of bird or beast or living thing, including, of course, human beings !

Again, anything pertaining to the manufacture or sale of intoxicating liquors or of narcotic or stimulating drugs, is to be shunned.

A word may not be amiss with regard to the injunction against becoming a professional soldier. The nature and the art of war are not regarded with favour by the Buddhist. But that does not mean, of course, that no measures may be taken by any individual or nation against aggression.

An apocryphal story told of the Buddha illustrates this point rather humorously.

There was a snake who, having heard that the Buddha taught living creatures not to kill or hurt one another, decided to follow this precept. One day whilst crossing a road, he was seen by a number of small boys who immediately began pelting him with stones. Remembering the Buddha's teaching he did not strike at the children who ceased not their cruel pastime until they left him for dead by the roadside. As it happened, the Buddha, accompanied by a retinue of bhikkhus was travelling the same road and, coming upon the sorely bruised and bleeding creature, inquired into the cause of the poor snake's pitiful condition. "I but followed Thy precept, Lord!" replied the snake, and told the Buddha what had occurred. Whereupon the Buddha answered: "It is true that I teach the doctrine of harmlessness, and you did act rightly in not wishing to hurt any of these children. But you might have hissed a little!"

Thus we see that the Buddhist, though pacific, is not necessarily a pacifist, in the social sense of the word!

In summing up the second or ethical section of the Noble Eightfold Path, comprising Right Speech, Right Action and Right Livelihood, we may say, then, that its general purport is to raise us from being human to being humane!

The Mental Triplicity: Having discussed to some extent the triplicity of behaviour, we now come to the triplicity of mental and spiritual activity: Right Endeavour, Right Recollectedness and Right Rapture.

Right Endeavour is classed as a mental activity since any kind of endeavour from which the mental element has been abstracted or in which it is not represented to the fullest possible extent, cannot be properly classed as such. Whatever energy is expended in the effort must be intelligently directed, and the more intelligent is the direction, the closer the approach to Right Endeavour.

There are four main efforts which constitute Right Endeavour. They are: (1) The effort to prevent the arising of new states of bondage; (2) The effort to check the progress of existing states of bondage; (3) The effort to bring about new tendencies to freedom; (4) The effort to enhance existing tendencies to freedom. Bondage to what? Bondage to suffering! Freedom from what? Freedom from suffering! The Buddhist never shuts his eyes to suffering: he stares it out of countenance!

How do we prevent the arising of new states of bondage? By not engendering new cravings. And how do we check the progress of existing states of bondage? By ridding ourselves of present cravings. How do we bring about new tendencies to freedom? By ridding ourselves of present cravings. And how do we enhance existing tendencies to freedom? By not engendering new cravings! It is all surprisingly simple to understand; if we but mind it!

The Right Endeavour of the Buddhist, then, is primarily a mental process, turning the mind in the desired direction away from the undesirable, the direction of craving. To do so it requires but a little thinking on our part, a little self-discussion concerning the sorrow-bringing consequences of dwelling upon our desires, our yearnings; of clinging to the passing, the temporary; of attachment to the perishable, the vanishing! "Vanity of vanities! all is vanity!" said a wise king.

And then, with the mind turned in the right direction, all the energy which we expend must of necessity turn in that direction also, for there is then no other outlet. The effort required, therefore, does not so much lie in the energy spent as in the path along which it spends itself. To keep the mind turned in the proper direction, *that* is Right Endeavour; and there is no reason why the mind should not be as well-controlled an instrument as is the hand or the foot! We must transform the mind from a prancing, undirected colt into a spirited, well-broken steed.

Next in order is Right Recollectedness, the capacity to see things as they really are, that mental faculty contributing most to Right

Understanding. The nature of men's minds is to mix new perceptions with old recollections, so that every fact we observe is immediately coloured by the actual contents of our mind. When interpreting a new observation we do not rely upon the facts supplied by that particular perception so much as upon our preconceived notions, habits of thought, prejudices and suppositions.

Now Right Recollectedness is the cultivation of that faculty which makes it its business to see things in their own light rather than in that of our mind's providing, to listen to what the fact has to say about itself rather than to what we have to say about the fact.

This it is not an easy thing to accomplish. It requires very considerable practice and the constant recollection to be awake to the fact as such, instead of to that conglomeration of mental residue we so proudly refer to as our mind, which clothes each perception in fanciful attire giving it fictitious value in its relation to other facts that have been similarly distorted.

By facts we really refer to those states physical, sensational and mental, consequent upon impressions from without, evoked either directly or indirectly. To account to oneself accurately and completely what is happening at each successive moment of experience, that is Right Recollectedness. A fact goes no further than its effect upon us, no further than the response it is able to evoke. And whether that response be on the part of the body only, such as upon a pin prick; or emotional, such as upon a bereavement; or mental, such as upon the reading of a book; or a combination of any two or all three of these states, fundamentally makes no difference whatsoever. A fact is a fact only in so far as it succeeds in calling forth from us a response.

In the exercise of recollectedness it is that response, then, that we must analyze, dissect into its proper constituents: see whence it comes, whereunto it leads, what factors it calls into play, how vital these are, and, more especially, to what extent it has to be considered apart from the mental associations we bring to bear upon it. For it is these associations which contribute most to giving any fact fictitious worth. When I see a cat, I immediately associate this visual notion with my entire previous experience of cats in general; with what I have heard and read about them; with other domestic animals; with wild animals to which they are related; with people whose character is cat-like; with the sensations produced by these various experiences; until the entire content of my mental nature is stirred in response to this retinal impression. My judgment in reference to that particular cat is therefore unbalanced: it is unfair to the cat, and unjust to the actual situation. It is that which we must recollect: we must learn to respond to actual conditions rather than to an haphazard impression inextricably mixed up with past haphazard impressions. And the practice of Right Recollectedness will so purify our mind and stimulate our understanding that with every successful step taken along that line of thinking there pervades our nature a feeling of rapturousness which will amply compensate us for whatever efforts we may have made, for thus we know that we are no longer deceived by mere appearances and impressions.

This finally brings us to the last step upon the Noble Eightfold Path, namely Right Rapture. But this is so difficult a thing to discuss, that only actual experience can give us the least inkling into its meaning. This Rapture indeed is "peace that passeth understanding" the mere mental analysis of which carries with it little conviction. The mind becomes tranquillized, not being subject any longer to the constant danger of being brought to the boiling point by the flaring up into passion of smouldering embers of craving, yearning, and desire. It becomes lucid and serene, clear and reflective. And with it, also that with which it comes into contact, the world, becomes clarified and translucent. Instead of looking *at* things, or even *into* things, the mind begins to look *through* things. It does not any longer have to solve problems, because it dissolves them. The joy that accompanies such a state of mind simply beggars description. A faint and sporadic glimpse of this condition is sufficient to make one prepared to sacrifice everything of pleasure one has ever known for the sake of another such experience.

And then to think not only that such a state of mind can be attained to again from time to time, but that it can actually become a permanent mental attribute to an extent compared to which such a first touch was but the merest glimmer! That is Right Rapture!

However, there are many other kinds of rapturous states of mind which it is easy to mistake for that induced by *Right* Rapture in its earlier stages. The main drawback to these is that, though ecstatic in effect, they will not lead to the more permanent condition referred to. They hold the same relation to the Right Rapture of the Buddhist as an artificial stimulation holds to a naturally vigorous state. Sooner or later they will produce a corresponding reaction as painful as the ecstasy was delightful. They may be recognized chiefly by the mental confusion with which they are accompanied and to which they give rise, by the insistence on the part of their victim upon some fanatical notion, and more particularly by the exaltation of his self-importance. Cases of false rapture are often the result of religious revivals and accompany so-called conversions. Also sensuous delights may give rise to false rapture. From the Buddhist point of view all such conditions are more in the nature of intoxications than of true rapture. Right Rapture invariably clarifies and tranquillizes the mind and minimizes the feeling of self: that is its chief token.

No wonder then that the Buddhist who has once had the first taste of this condition begins to regard the body with contempt and to look upon it as a fetter to the continuous enjoyment of Right Rapture. For it is the distraction of the senses that stands in the way. He therefore makes every possible effort to subdue the senses so that they shall not any longer constitute a hindrance. He begins to recognize that mere sense-enjoyment cannot begin to compensate for the loss of one moment's true rapture. The very thought of sense pleasures is as ridiculous to him as the thought of a lollipop is to a professor of mathematics!

And by sense-pleasures is not meant merely the actual employment of the senses at such times. Any recollection of such pleasures accompanied by the least clinging thereto and craving therefor and yearning thereafter is quite as much of a distraction as is the actual sense enjoyment. The same holds good for all fabrications of the imagination having sense delights as a basis.

But sensuous craving is only one of the obstacles in the way of experiencing Right Rapture. There are others, such as resentment and ill-will, pride, mistaken notions concerning the nature of the self, hesitancy, longing for existence material or immaterial, dependence upon ritual and ceremonial, envy and self-righteousness, and, of course, ignorance. All these are stones around the necks of those who wish to rise to the heights of sublime rapture, preventing us in great measure from even obtaining a mere foretaste of what may be in store for us.

What may be in store for us is Nibbana, that state of liberation whence there is no return to bondage, in which there is no vestige of self-feeling left, and only bliss remains. Nibbana is the end and aim of the Noble Eightfold Path. There is no higher goal, either for god or man. In so far as it can be called a condition at all, it is one of perfect equilibrium in which experience and the thing experienced are fully united leaving no strain whatsoever to be adjusted, no kamma to be generated or reduced. And Nibbana, once attained, is attained For Ever!

THE SOUL

WHAT to the oriental mind is an axiom—the persistence of the human entity and its repeated embodiment—to the western mind has to be proven. This is not to be wondered at in view of the fact that we of the pale races are taught to believe only that which we can physically demonstrate, with the exception, of course, of theological dogma which we are ordered obediently to reiterate on dire penalties of soul!

The oriental mind is somewhat differently constituted from ours. It is not as matter of fact on the one hand, and on the other not as credulous: in addition, it is considerably more logical and subtle. Hence it sees as facts what we often view as superstitions, and it smilingly rejects dogmas that to the minds of many of us have sacred value.

It is a little known, yet an established, fact that the eye of the more primitive races is sharper than ours, but is unable to distinguish as many shades of colour. The American Indian, for example, can see at least one-tenth as much further than can the average man of our own race. Also he sees objects more sharply defined, because his vision depends more on contrast between light and dark than on colour distinctions. The higher colours—those beyond the blue in the spectrum—are all blue to him: he cannot clearly distinguish indigo, violet, lavender and purple. Again the crude, primitive colours appeal to him most because those he can properly see and appreciate.

Now it may be that there is a similar relation between the western mind and the oriental, as there is between the quality of vision of the more primitive man and that of ourselves. We see colour distinctions that the American aborigine cannot appreciate: so the easterner may see logical subtleties where we see but quibbles. We may see facts in sharper outline: he sees them more harmoniously blended.

In judging mental conceptions coming to us from the east we do well to bear this comparison in mind, especially where religious and philosophical concepts are concerned.

All religions, without exception, teach the persistence of the human entity. We may distinguish, however, three different classes of this concept:

(1) In the first class we may include those religions which assume that a creator brings forth a new soul each time a child is born. The child, placed in a certain environment, grows to maturity

and in the few years of its existence as a human being is supposed to decide for itself its fate during the remainder of eternity. Theological apologetics has to step in to harmonize such a ridiculous and truly wicked conception with the natural reasonableness of the human mind. It has to prove that, however unequal the lot of different human beings may be here below, a certain kind of Providence will see to it that this "apparent" injustice is rectified in the course of the eternal existence following this life. Whatever problem may present itself, such as what happens to the souls of children dying before their first or seventh or twelfth year of life, is simply disposed of by a pious commonplace. Why there are the blind and the wretched and the crippled and the criminally inclined, is answered in the same fashion: similarly why these poor souls at the hands of their Creator receive their punishment first and a possible reward only in the hereafter, according to the meekness and patience with which they may have borne their undeserved afflictions. It is easy to multiply such knotty questions pertaining to this class of the soul concept.

(2) The second class comprises those religions which suppose the persistence of the soul to be managed in a much more efficient manner. They postulate an original creation of souls in the far distant past, which at first are but dimly conscious of their separation from the Godhead but gradually

are becoming immersed in the coarser kinds of substances until they embody more or less conglomerately that kind of material which we know as minerals. And having reached this lowest level of to us manifest existence they manage to climb back again, by means of an evolutionary process, through the vegetable, animal, human and progressive angel kingdoms to the very Godhead Who in the first instance created them. But they are supposed to return as individually developed souls bringing back with them the experience and perhaps the memory of their long exile in the nether regions. What might be the purpose of such a lengthy and painful pilgrimage, however, has yet to be explained, unless indeed we may regard the statement of its being so as an explanation. When the question is put as to what benefit a perfect Godhead might derive from separating part of himself in order that the first part, through contact with the second part, may return to Him split up into individual consciousnesses, there is either silence or else the supposition is advanced that the Godhead Himself is growing and evolving and that the cumulative experience of the returning souls adds to his own experience. But then we are again left in the dark as to what he does with all this experience which he has been so busy gathering during those innumerable æons that eternity has been going on, except play the same game over and over again unceasingly! We are also confronted with the question: "How is it that, having had eternities innumerable of experience behind him, the Godhead has not yet succeeded in making men more perfect than they are to-day, in fact, has not yet succeeded in creating a world without suffering?"

Of the two sets of theories—both of which may sharpen our ingenuity in attempting to account for God's purpose—the latter not only gives us more mental exercise, but establishes many more accurate facts regarding man than does the former. However, whereas the second theory merely leaves us in the dark concerning the aims and purposes of the Deity, the first set leaves us mentally in *total* obscurity as regards the facts touching both human and divine manifestation!

(3) The third class of religion deals with facts only, ascertainable facts, that is to say. It confines itself to knowledge obtained by some, obtainable by all. It represents the Religion of Science, the Science of Religion, the Knowledge obtained by the Buddha when he attained Nibbana. This class is confined to Buddhism; to be more exact, to Hinayana Buddhism, or Theravada, the Teaching of the Elders!

Now the first class of religions comprise the religions of faith with regard to God and haphazard theories with regard to Man; the second class those of faith with regard to God combined with some knowledge with regard to Man; the third class comprises only Buddhism which is a religion of knowledge concerning both Deity and Man.

And which is that knowledge concerning Man common to both the second class of religions (Hinduism, Gnosticism, Theosophy) and the third class (Buddhism)? Primarily it is knowledge concerning the persistence of the human individual before the present earth life, during the same, and after it. It is knowledge not based on theory, but on actual experience; not the experience by a few only, but the experience of a great number amongst mankind, and subject to experimental verification.

It is *of* no value whatever in our exposition of the Buddhist view of the human soul to compare unreasonable theories with reasonable ones. We shall therefore ignore those theological surmises belonging to the religions in class one, and confine ourselves to those which at least attempt to do justice to the inherent capacities of the human mind!

The conception of the human soul held by the religions in class two accounts for human existence by assuming that it has gradually evolved through immense periods of time ensouling in sequence the mineral, the vegetable, the animal, and finally the human forms. It distinguishes between the evolution of the form and the evolution of the consciousness inhabiting the form; the consciousness progressing from lower to higher forms; the forms themselves becoming more and more expressive of the consciousnesses ensouling them. The urge towards progression of both form and consciousness is supplied by a Deity which, for some reason or other, desires this process to take place in order to gain divine experience through his creation as part of himself.

Having lingered for æons of time in the mineral kingdom, the consciousnesses, according to these religious philosophies, become less conglomerate as they advance into the vegetable realm. Yet they have to remain here during a very considerable period until they are ready to emerge, this time as more definite entities, in the animal world. But even here the entities are not definite enough to live separate existences. As they advance from the lower to the higher animals, less of the same kind will belong to one, "group-soul," until finally only two or three dogs, or cats, or elephants, may constitute one soul-entity. These, coming into close contact with the human element, may at last break apart and reach separate soul-existence after which, when their time for re-birth arrives, they will be born as primitive human beings with strong tendencies towards conglomerate existence, expressing itself in tribal and family ties. The progress through the human kingdom is very much quicker than it was in the preceding realms, yet this period alone may be reckoned in millions of years!

It is this human stage of the progression which interests us most at the present time, seeing that we are occupying it just now. But we are not to lose sight of the fact that this process of "creation," of "evolution," is going on now as much as it ever did. The divine life is supposed to be constantly urging forward through the kingdoms of nature, of which we are conscious mainly of the mineral, vegetable, animal and human. Mineral life is constantly merging into plant life, that into animal existence, this again into human being, which in turn becomes angel life. There is a perpetual progression, without beginning, without end!

Now the Buddhist conception of the persistence of the individual entity substantially agrees with the above summary which may be studied in detail in modern Theosophical literature and which, to the western mind, will appeal as a highly logical and reasonable sequence of events. The main difference between this and the Buddhist view lies in the fact that, whereas the Hindu, the Gnostic, or the Theosophist starts out with a concept concerning a Deity unaccounted for upon which he hinges his view of the world around him, the Buddhist begins with the *Here and Now*, even as a man just aroused from sleep first looks about himself!

The Buddhist does not deny the existence of Deity, but he looks upon it as an individual entity as limited in consciousness and experience *in its own realm* as the human entity is in this. He certainly does not regard it as an ultimate Godhead: of such a concept Buddhism is not guilty.

Where the sole aim and purpose of human existence from the Hindu, the Gnostic, the Theosophical point of view is a reunion with the Deity whence the human soul is supposed to have sprung, such a reunion has no meaning to the Buddhist other than constituting an entrance upon another series of existences as impermanent and as productive of suffering from that level as is the human series from this. And this reunion with Deity which is the key-note of the other conceptions mentioned *must by no means be confused with the attainment by the Buddhist of Nibbana!*

Nor does the Buddhist regard the human soul as a very sharply defined entity. A permanent self to him is an impossibility, a contradiction in terms. The self changes from moment to moment physically, emotionally, mentally, and spiritually. We are not now what we were a second ago. Millions upon millions of changes have taken place in the atomic and molecular constitution of our self since we last thought of ourselves. True, we have a sense of continuity, a feeling of continuity, just as the retina of our eye has the faculty of retaining the impression of a light-impact after the light itself has ceased. But even as we recognize that a flash of lightning is but a spark which we see as a broken line long after the spark has ceased to exist, so our sense of continuity should be regarded as a similar phenomenon which imparts a feeling of coherency and permanency where there are but disconnected impacts.

To the Buddhist, therefore, the persistence of the human entity is a persistence only in so far as there is a feeling of continuity. In so far as that feeling is broken, there is no persistence, no "soul"; in so far as such a feeling governs us—whether it be but as an instinct or an inborn tendency, or as a visualization or a memory—there is persistence.

In view of this explanation how can we maintain that a human entity after awakening from sleep in the morning is the same human entity as that which went to sleep the night before? On the other hand, how can we maintain that it is not? For the break in continuity has not been long enough or strong enough entirely to obliterate all tendency to recollection of previous happenings. We have added something to our capacity to respond due to the experiences of the day before. We have abated somewhat our desire to respond, due to the same experiences. We have changed the controls, so to speak.

Similarly, there is a great deal of difference between an infant, and the person that has grown up from that infant. Is it the same person? Hardly! Is it a different person? Hardly! It is the same in so far as there is a sense of continuity, physical, emotional, or mental. It is different in so far as any portion of continuity has been obliterated.

And when we come to apply this to the period elapsing between death in one existence and birth in the next, we have exactly the same condition to deal with, with the exception, perhaps, that it is a somewhat less familiar situation to the minds of many of us, because the sense of continuity has to reach out over what we consider, from our limited point of view, a very large space of time. But in comparison it is no larger than that between evening and morning!

We now can understand the confusion of non-Buddhist translators and writers whenever the subject of soul is mentioned in Buddhist literature where at one time the existence of a soul seems to be denied, only to be implied again in the next sentence!

There is still another point in which the Buddhist conception of the progress of the entity materially differs from that put forward by the religions represented in the second class. In the latter the urge towards progression is supplied by a fundamental Deity intent upon vicarious

* 5

experience, and the sole aim and purpose of human advancement along the evolutionary path is the satisfaction of divine desire. But to the Buddhist desire in all its aspects, whether human or divine, cannot but be productive of suffering. The Deity in point is a macroscopic entity, as much subject to birth, death and decay as is the human entity here. We are cells in its body, subject to the processes taking place therein, just as we, in turn, constitute a deity to the cells in our body which similarly are subject to the human activities. What to our human consciousness is a few seconds, to the consciousness inherent in our body cells represents millions upon millions of years, whole cycles of evolution. Even so, what to us are æons upon æons of time, to the macroscopic consciousness in whose body we for the moment participate, are but seconds or minutes of time experience.

Now from the Buddhist point of view it is quite within the limits of possibility so to expand our consciousness as to actually participate in the consciousness of the Deity of which we form part, and though for the time being such an expansion of consciousness (cosmic consciousness, it has been called) is a truly wonderful experience in so far as it gives us a sense of the utter insignificance of the common human course of events, it does not put an end to suffering: on the contrary, it substitutes the great suffering of the Deity for the comparatively light suffering of the man. We may grasp this perhaps a little better if we consider that this entire world system, including the total amount of bitterness, pain, and distress to be found therein, is but the manifest existence of one single macrocosmic entity amongst innumerable of his compeers; and when our consciousness becomes expanded to the extent suggested, after the first rapture over the fact of this expansion has subsided we must necessarily, without in any way being able to relieve it, participate in that greater agony when it is so much more difficult to withdraw!

Understanding this, the Buddhist draws a sharp distinction between the reunion with the Deity, and the attainment of Nibbana wherein *only* permanent extinction of suffering can be found!

Neither does the urge towards continued existence generate entirely within the divine body in which each one of us is but a particle. True, it may give us the initial impulse: not so much as an act of creation, however, than as a natural event incidental to its own continued existence; a process of reflection, perhaps. But as soon as this has taken place, desire in its most primitive form—attraction—sets in and it is this which leads us on through form upon form, from consciousness to consciousness, until finally the futility of it all dawns upon us and we seek for a way out. This sense of futility, however, cannot reach us until we have well advanced into the human kingdom where we can organize the first attempt towards an escape from this prison of desires. And the Buddha appeared at the very period when many of our present humanity were in a measure ready to make this escape. He was not the first Buddha to appear: previous Buddhas were ready to point out the Path to Escape at corresponding periods in the progression of previous humanities, humanities that have advanced—in so far as they did not avail themselves of their Buddhas' counsel—into the kingdoms beyond the present human realm, those of the angels and archangels and gods. Similarly another Buddha will be ready to give the same teaching to the humanity to follow ours, the members of which are now still largely within the present animal realm. As there is no end to the procession of humanities, so there is no end to the procession of Buddhas each one of which appears at the psychological time.

As already suggested, it is by no means necessary for us to avail ourselves of our Buddha's counsel. If we do, we shall attain Nibbana, that condition of freedom from stress and distress whence we need never emerge again. If we do not, we continue our evolutionary process towards godhood through the various gradations leading thereto, and as we pass through each subsequent kingdom we shall have another opportunity to listen to the next Buddha's teaching until finally we shall be ready to avail ourselves of it. Thus it is that each Buddha is designated as the Teacher of both Gods and Men; that each humanity has its Buddha; that, as evolution proceeds, there will be more and more entities that will strive to attain Nibbana, leaving fewer and fewer of those that once were human beings to populate the divine regions.

Thus it can also be understood why desire, particularly the desire for selfhood, is the basis of all manifestation, more especially that of the gods. For it is they who have, time after time, from kingdom to kingdom, refused to let go of their insistence upon self, having clung to I-ness as the only thing worth while to them. But as they advanced it became increasingly difficult for them to extract themselves from the region of their manifest existence. Whereas in the human kingdom, after insight sets in, the attainment of Nibbana may be a matter of a few years only, at most of a few more lives; in each subsequent realm this attainment becomes more and more thwarted on account of the greater complexities of attending circumstances surrounding the entity; just as a king has more difficulties to overcome, more forms to go through, more explanations to make upon leaving his kingdom, than one of his subjects to leave his abode. The king would have to wind up his affairs at great length: the plain subject would not have so many affairs to wind up.

Thus it is that, whenever a Buddha appears in order to urge humanity to take steps towards the attainment of Nibbana the very gods, knowing how much more difficult this attainment will be at their level, assist the Buddha's efforts in every way possible both for their own and for mankind's emancipation. We have the story of the God Sakka, the presiding Deity of the world system to which we belong, upon Gotama's attaining Buddhahood when the latter was deliberating whether He could persuade mankind of the practical value of the Middle Path, imploring the Buddha to present His teaching to the world for the sake of both gods and men.

We have seen, then, that in a certain sense the persistence of the human entity is a fact in nature ; that at a certain point in the human stage it has its first choice to continue along the road of desire or to follow the path of desirelessness ; that this choice presents itself again at the corresponding stages in the subsequent kingdoms as each Buddha appears, but that at each subsequent presentation it is more difficult to disentangle oneself from one's ties ; that the advancement along the road to godhood involves wider consciousness, wider desires, wider responsibilities, wider suffering ; and that each subsequent realm contains fewer ex-human entities than the previous mainly due to the entering into Nibbana of those gods that reach the fruit of enlightenment.

We will now turn our attention to the repeated rebirths of the entity whilst in the human stage.

Rebirth.—It must be understood that from the Buddhist point of view there is nothing in the human soul that is a perduring something—such as a divine spark or a special soul creation—which is the permanent transmigrator from one form to another. It is this very concept which the Buddhist strenuously combats for the reason that such a false notion concerning the existence of a fundamental self constitutes the greatest obstacle to the attainment of Nibbana. The belief in a permanent soul entity, if held as a cardinal dogma, causes our actions to be based upon it, which is detrimental to the principal achievement aimed at by the Buddhist. There is chain of continuity, however, running from any one stage of the existence of an entity to any subsequent stage, a chain made up of separate links held together by our sense of continuity; but there is not an unchangeable spark or a perduring soul running *along* this chain. The chain in point, like a ray of light or a current of water, does not serve as a bridge to an entity: it simply constitutes that entity.

Now when a man dies he is immediately reborn in another sphere of existence. He has not altogether vanished, gone up into nothingness; nor has he been translated to an eternal hell or heaven! Modern spiritualism, corroborating the claims of the ancients, has shown us that under certain conditions it even is possible for him to establish communication with the world he has recently left. In the terminology of the Theosophist, he is now living on the Astral Plane. The Buddhist does not exactly put it that way. To him the man has been reborn either in a pleasant state or in an unpleasant state, according to conditions he has set up during the time of his recent physical existence, which itself was a similar consequence. Some of these states are exceedingly painful; some of them very delightful; and both the Theosophist and the Spiritualist will agree with such a view. To call the unpleasant conditions Hells, and the pleasant ones Heavens, might serve the purpose if it were not that these words have been subjected to so much theological juggling as to arouse more prejudice than understanding. At any rate, into whichever condition the human entity is reborn at the termination of his earth life, it must, like the former, come to an end sooner or later. The Buddhist does not subscribe to either an eternal hell or an eternal heaven!

In the new stage upon which he has just entered the man passes through similar conditions as he did here, that is to say through a period of awakening, corresponding to infancy; through one of adaptation, corresponding to childhood and youth; through one of vigorous activity, corresponding to manhood; and finally through one of decline, which corresponds to old age. And when at last he is ready to pass out of that existence, by very virtue of the energy he had stored up he is once more attracted to and reborn in this physical world, where he passes through the same general stages as he did before.

This process continues unintermittently like the motion of the pendulum of a clock until he himself discovers the force that keeps the clock wound and the pendulum swinging, and is willing to exert himself to counteract that force. He learns that it is his cravings that keep him upon this eternal grind, and that, by ceasing to add additional cravings to the fever of existence it will gradually subside until he finally reaches the perfect balance of Nibbana, just as a man, when he finds that a fire is kept alive by the addition of new fuel, can let the fire burn itself out by refusing to add more fuel. The flames will not subside immediately: there is still enough of the old fuel to keep them going for a while. But if he persistently refuses to put in more, they *must* cease sooner or later!

The reason why the Buddhist does not speak of material existence upon earth with an interlude in a superphysical region, is simply because this gives an entirely wrong impression of what is really going on. Both kinds of existences are equally material and, roughly speaking, they are both on earth. The matter may differ in quality, but not in materiality. It is this difference in quality which makes it difficult for the person in one stage of existence to be aware of the other stage, just as it is not possible for the colourblind man to see different shades. The light vibrations are all around him and affect his retina, but he cannot respond as can the normal person, and therefore does not see colours similarly. It is not by any means impossible, however, to acquire the faculty of responding to the material of the "intermediate" world as perfectly as to that of the world in which we function for the moment. Many persons make special efforts to do so and quite often succeed. But the Buddhist regards this kind of exercise usually as a waste of energy: the same amount of energy expended in mastering some craving or other seems to him to be much more profitable. It is the difference between wrong endeavour and Right Endeavour!

It is often contended by those who, with the Buddhist, believe in rebirth that a man reincarnates "in order to get experience". From the Buddhist point of view this is a fallacy. He does not take birth to get experience, but *to become surfeited with experience*, which is quite a different matter. True, he gets the experience he has been craving for, whether it be pleasant or otherwise, together with the consequences attendant upon his cravings, which is more than he bargained for in the first instance. And from that standpoint he may be said to become more perfect ; not more perfect in godliness, as our friends the reincarnationists have it, but more perfect in selflessness, seeing that all insistence upon self leads him further and further into the mire of woe. He gradually learns what kinds of desires he is to avoid most, and how he can succeed in extinguishing craving. The impermanency of any condition of happiness affects him in a way which makes him ask whether there is not a permanent state of contentment—not one just a little more permanent, a little longer heaven ; but bliss enduring forever. It is not until he is thus affected that Buddhism begins to have any attraction for him. As long as he still is satisfied with the changeable emptiness around him, with aimlessness of gathering facts like a child collecting shells at the sea shore, so long the religion of the Buddha can only offer him protection from pitfalls and deep places by suggesting that it is productive of less suffering if he does the things that are right rather than those that are wrong, if he follows the unselfish rather than the selfish course of action, if he is generous rather than greedy, if he cultivates a loveable disposition rather than a surly one. It will make it easier for him to enter upon the Path to Liberation, once he decides to do so, by not encumbering himself with too much desire fuel.

Neither does the Buddhist concern himself quite so much with the mechanics of the process of rebirth as do the other believers in reincarnation. It is of more importance to him to know how to surmount the necessity of rebirth than how exactly the process of rebirth takes place. His attitude is psychological rather than mechanical. He prefers to ride in his vehicle to taking it apart.

There is more than one good reason for this preference. It is so easy to lose sight of the broad aim when we get mentally involved in so-called scientific details! Also the latter give rise to differences in opinion according to the power of observation of different investigators and the weight attached to each fact in the process; and the resultant discussion is endless. Besides, the mere collecting of data on any subject is no aid towards the Great Emancipation. Then, the processes themselves differ somewhat according to individual peculiarities, and a great deal according to the period in which they take place, both as regards the period in the history of the race and in the history of the world system to which we belong. The fundamental facts, those with which Buddhism primarily deals, do not vary: the attendant circumstances which govern the mechanical manifestation of these facts change from cycle to cycle, aye, from century to century. Again, at a certain stage along the Noble Eightfold

Path it becomes possible for us to see for ourselves, if we wish to do so, how any particular process in nature takes its course, whether it refers to the life after death ; to rebirth ; the constitution of the earth ; the existence of the gods ; the nature of light ; events of the past, at a distance, in the future ; or anything else that may be required, by simply turning our attention in that particular direction. Our mind becomes like a searchlight illuminating any subject towards which it is directed and upon which it is allowed to play. Whether we shall avail ourselves of those faculties at that time, is another story. There may be other things in which we may be more interested, things of the portent of which we may have at present not even an inkling.

The Buddha does not expect every one immediately to follow the precepts leading to Nibbana : He knows human nature too well. To those to whom this path does not appeal he makes it clear that they can, by following the gentler courses of action, at any rate prepare for themselves the happier kinds of future existences. By subduing the coarser desires they can be reborn into states of light and splendour, of joy and godliness, the abodes of angels. By selfishly indulging the animal passions they will be reborn into conditions dismal and dreary, where there is confusion and prolonged suffering, veritable hells ; and time hangs heavy there. But when the energies that landed them in either state have exhausted themselves, their rebound must of necessity take them back into this sphere of existence under such conditions as are appropriate to their general responsiveness. In this way they are continually working up supplies of energy to be exhausted as soon as the opportunity for their release presents itself, and they thus go on for birth after birth until they too shall experience that sense of futility which is a prerequisite to treading the Path to Liberation

Under normal conditions it may be said that once born into the human kingdom there is no retrogression back into the animal. The few exceptions upon which stress is laid in Buddhist writings as particular examples have so taken hold of the imagination of our critics that the most absurd notions concerning our belief in rebirth have filtered through to the people in western countries! Before such retrogression can take place the most selfish and destructive kinds of existence must have been led for a good many births, until finally no vestige of human nature is left. But as long as there still is a tendency to humanness, so long must one naturally gravitate to human existence. It is the law of Conservation of Energy as applied to human continuity. That which we store up by way of craving must become inherent as instinct or tendency, and lead to particular externalizations. This holds good under any and all circumstances. So with those of rebirth: our inherent cravings draw us forward from birth to birth into conditions of our own making, however much we might like to withdraw from the bargain in the later light of wider knowledge.

Thus we have before us the choice between three courses of action: between indulging the coarser cravings generating the kind of energy that impels us towards states of indescribable misery; or favouring the more æsthetic sense pleasures which stimulate the higher creative faculties, that bring conditions of heavenly delight which, however prolonged, are still ephemeral; or recognizing all sense entanglement of whatever description, whether productive of pain or pleasure, whether resulting in low states or high, whether leading to unfavourable or propitious rebirths, as so much entanglement that ultimately *must* be unravelled and deciding, therefore, that the sooner we begin doing so the less we shall have to disentangle, in other words grasping the teaching of the Blessed Buddha aright by resolving to tread the Noble Eightfold Path!

KAMMA

SINCE in our language we have no single word that can cover the full meaning of the word "kamma," we have to retain it in our exposition of Buddhist philosophy with an appropriate explanation. We must not forget in doing so that, though Buddhist ethics may be advanced at whatever stage of mental capacity—and their loftiness is hardly equalled by the ethics of any other religion—Buddhist philosophy is for the mature mind or that maturing.

The usual English rendering of kamma is "cause and effect" or "action and reaction". The better way to think of this concept, however, is to regard it as rebound, reaction, or better still, perhaps, as organic responsiveness, interaction, or adjustment. Let us explain.

Any event of whatever nature that takes place is the outcome of more or less conflicting forces. If I throw a ball, I am setting in motion a very complex set of forces: those of my mind, my muscles, my senses; those inherent in the ball, in its shape, its substance, its size; those of the atmosphere; of gravitation; in fact, all the forces of the universe assist in my throwing of the ball. They act upon, and interact amongst themselves in acting upon, the ball and its thrower.

Now it is to the extent that I unbalance the forces of nature, as I do by throwing the ball, that sooner or later I also become subject to the process of rebalancement. For it is the disturbed balance of forces which constitutes the Universe and it is their continuously thwarted attempts at balancement that bring about things as we know them, that create the worlds and make them go round. We ourselves are parts of these forces, and in so far as we have individually aided in contributing to their disturbance, we must also in like measure assist at their readjustment. It is this individual participation in such readjustment that is called "kamma".

The forces of nature are both destructive and constructive at the same time. The plant grows by decomposing the soil, by destroying old cells and building new ones, just as we build houses by destroying rocks and trees, and shaping stones, boards and beams. Nature always tends to maintain a balance. If a beam is lifted at one end, a corresponding pressure is exercised by the other end. The cosmic forces are not in balance for the same reason that the air is never perfectly still or the sea perfectly quiet. If once a universal balance were reached, the forces would have ceased to be forces. They are what they are through sheer unbalancement, resulting in motion, friction, interaction, adjustment. But such ultimate balance can be reached as little as the figure 0·999 . . . can ever become 1, or the figure 0·000 . . . 1 become zero.

Contrary to all other religious philosophies, Buddhism does not ask the question how in the first instance this unbalancing of forces originated. Whether it ever had a beginning, is one of those futile speculations that distract the mind from the main point at issue, namely: "Seeing that this unbalanced condition exists, to what extent does it affect us, and in what degree can we withdraw from its influence?" In other words, taking for granted the undeniable fact, we deal with it rather than speculate concerning it.

When we are being awakened by the magic touch of Buddhist thought and are impelled to look about ourselves, we first realize that we are prey to numerous forces about us. We do not deny the fact of our existence, nor follow the ostrich policy of burying our heads in the sand of the desert of faith. We do not endeavour to place upon the shoulders of another being either the fact of our existence or the distress with which our existence is bound up. We recognize that there is suffering, and too much of it; that we are subject to it; that we are contributing to it; that we must cease to contribute to it; and that, as we cease to contribute to it, it also ceases to affect us. We recognize that, of all the forces playing through us and about us, the force of craving is the one which to us human beings holds out the most alluring prospects and is bound to end in the bitterest disappointments. Acknowledging the existence of many forces, we give mental preponderance to the force of craving.

By our cravings we gradually form ourselves into magnets that attract particular things. But our drawing power is constantly counteracted by the withdrawing power of external nature. In this way a constant strain is maintained between the forces working through us and those working upon us. The way in which we bear up under that strain is our kamma, for it constitutes our action, our response, our capacity, our adjustment; in fact, our character. This holds good mentally, emotionally and spiritually as well as physically, for the forces at work are of all kinds and not physical only. We oppose the natural external pull for the simple reason that we pulled first. We may even say that the extent to which we succeed or fail in opposing this outside pull which tries to drag away from us what we have succeeded in incorporating with the self, constitutes our kamma, that it is that which at any moment adds to or detracts from the established individual. Kamma is the constant reminder that we are but borrowers, that our conquest is but a temporary one, that there is nothing that we can actually call *our own*!

But this is only one side of the picture. When gradually we begin to understand something about this law of impact and response it is part of our mental make-up that we should endeavour to manipulate it. We do this for the purpose of bringing about results pictured by our imagination and urged by our desire. We establish tendencies and habits calculated to bring at least temporary satisfaction to our cravings. We learn to control our responsiveness, to curb it, to become reserved, in order that we may not spend accumulated energy in an unprofitable direction. We may even go so far as to use part of our forces to restrain and even prevent the outrush of certain energies, and by bending these back upon ourselves to neutralize those energies that are on the point of spending themselves. In this way we may establish a certain amount of equilibrium, a balance of restraint, which will enable us to contemplate without disturbance the facts of nature and of human nature. Such neutralization of kamma is possible and is a practice required by those who wish to follow the Way of the Buddha and to find an escape out of this maze of seemingly uncontrollable forces that influence and surround us on all sides.

We are, then, by no means blind playthings of blind forces; we are not just pieces of driftwood cast hither and thither upon the ocean of life. On the contrary, neither are we blind, nor are the forces with which we have to deal. We are filled with consciousness as the ocean is full of water. Each cell in our make-up has a consciousness of its own that is not dependent upon the consciousness of the self. The forces that play around the cells of our body, that proceed from us through our actions, our thoughts and our feelings; through our care, our food and our activity; through our habits, our impulses and our responses; these forces hold the same relations to the cells composing our system, as the forces with which we have to deal hold with regard to us. For we are but cells in a greater self-system. If we could but see ourselves reduced in size to such an extent as thoroughly to condense our appearance *together with its auric emanations*, we would see nothing essentially different from what we observe when contemplating the appearance of a cell under the microscope. If we could enlarge a cell of a certain kind to our size and be responsive to its corresponding organization, we would discover a living, breathing, active and conscious entity, not very unlike ourselves. That portion of ourselves which we call the body corresponds to the nucleus of the cell, and the surrounding matter to the circumference would become so rare through the process of enlarging that it would cease to be noticeable to our kind of sight, corresponding to what is called the human aura.

If once we are able to grasp this old principle—often put in the well-known Hermetic measure "As above, so below"—at the same time understanding that there is no advantage in the attainment of the next higher unit-consciousness, and realizing that there is a method of side-stepping this eternal procession, this evolutionary deceit, we shall have reached the required attitude for the practice of the Buddha's teachings.

In speaking of kamma, then, we are dealing with forces which, though not individually conscious, yet have a conscious issue in so far as they are the direct outcome of the activity of the Greater Being in whose make-up we are but cell units and in whom, therefore, "we move and live and have our being".

As ever, we have several courses of action before us in regard to these forces. We may let ourselves be swayed by them—drift with the stream, so to speak—at the same time trying to shield ourselves more or less from their severity, just as we seek protection from the inclemency of the weather by building shelter and wearing clothes, or as we seek forgetfulness of sorrow in drink, from worry in diversion. Again we may aid them—swim with the stream—by deliberately attuning ourselves as much as possible to the forces of nature, as when we harden our muscles and nerves, give social and patriotic aid, and endeavour to forward the Cause of Right. Or we may deliberately set ourselves against the impelling forces of nature in so far as they affect humankind—swim against the stream—as when we steal, or murder, or destroy, or enslave, or work our will on others. Or finally, we may endeavour to place ourselves outside the power of these forces to affect us in any way whatsoever—cross the stream of existence.

In all these cases we are manipulating kamma, but only in the last case we are manipulating it so that its influence becomes less and less, until finally no kamma is left. It is that condition in which kamma for us has utterly ceased, in which we have placed ourselves finally outside the influence of all disruptive forces—physical, emotional or mental, social or evolutional—that we shall have attained Nibbana. This is the aim the Buddhist sets before him. He neither aids nor hinders evolutionary progress; but if he *has* to choose between these two, he unhesitatingly aids. He does not advocate either social or anti-social doctrines; but if he *must* take issue, he favours those which do not disrupt the prevailing social organization. He does not even make it his business to seek out suffering for the sake of alleviating it; but where he finds it—and he finds it on all sides—he is ever willing to help, and at the same time to indicate the way in which in the future it may be prevented. He will never directly inflict suffering, not even for so-called "corrective purposes". He leaves that to Nature, he leaves that to Kamma. For where he can but pass judgment, Nature provides justice. Kamma will adjust all wrongs, will settle all disputes, will heal all wounds, will inflict all retribution; and we can only aid by opening man's inner vision, by making him understand that his present pain is of his own producing, that his present pleasure is at the expense of others, and that, as he is paying past debts by means of the former, so is he contracting new ones through the latter. Only the Middle Path, the Path of Neither Extreme, the Path of Peace, the Path of the Elders, can lead him from pain to contentment, from pleasure-seeking to the finding of true joy.

On the other hand it must be realized that it is not possible for us so to withdraw ourselves from the consequences of our former actions, thoughts and feelings that kamma will cease to affect us immediately. We still have so many consequences to endure that it may take many existences before we can reach a condition of final liberation. But as long as we are cheerfully willing to settle our debts, without contracting new ones through the accumulation of more stored-up energies through additional cravings, we shall slowly, but surely, attain Liberation. The old fuel must first burn itself out, and as we refuse to add more fuel to the fire of kamma, the fever of existence, must gradually abate.

The understanding of kamma is of no value to us except in so far as it affects the human entity. As an abstract cosmic principle it has no practical significance. Like all other Buddhist principles it is a practical and personal one, We must make ourselves perfectly responsive to all impacts from without to which we intend to respond, whether they be physical, mental, or emotional, in order to establish the necessary adjustment of our faculties.

The Nature of Adjustment: Kamma is inextricably interwoven with consciousness, awareness. Wherever there is awareness, there must be at the same time an adjustment of our faculties. If the adjustment has been successfully accomplished and there is no further effort involved, the awareness ceases and the call for response has been answered.

Now if this adjustment of our faculties can be accomplished without a great effort, the consciousness is agreeably affected, we enjoy pleasure ; but if a great effort is required on the part of our faculties to achieve adjustment, or if in spite of all effort on their part such adjustment is impossible, we have pain. For example, if a note is intoned and the hearing organism readily responds, we call the sound a pleasant one. If a shrill whistle is sounded which taxes the ear's capacity, the sound is far from pleasant. Should, however, either intonation continue at exactly the same pitch and volume, it does not take long for the ear to cease to respond : it may or may not have adjusted itself, but no call is made for further effort. So in all respects our emotional and our mental organizations act likewise.

Now in so far as there is inadequate reaction, or rather imperfect organic response, there is awareness ; where there is awareness, there is strain or unbalancement ; where there is unbalancement, there is the desire to adjust the lost balance ; where there is such desire there is entanglement ; and in so far as there is entanglement, there is kamma. Kamma is the web that we have woven into a separate self-conscious entity, and which has to be unravelled. It is a Gordian knot that cannot be cut, must be carefully untwisted ! How are we to go about it ?

Our organization is threefold : physical, emotional and mental. In reality so sharp distinctions can hardly be drawn : all three aspects are closely intertwined, but this analysis will serve for clearness' sake. In the course of our "entanglement," our "evolution" as modern parlance has it, the physical was the foundation of the emotional, and these two of the mental. The last of the three, the mental, has therefore to be unravelled first : we must start at the last stitch ! This can be done only by clarifying our understanding. Hence Buddhism as a mental process, a philosophy. And once attaining to Right

Understanding, the first step on the Noble Eightfold Path, our emotional and physical organizations can be taken care of in accordance with it.

It is of the utmost importance that this be rightly comprehended. For were we to try to begin with our emotional aspect, we would undoubtedly become crazy fanatics; were we to try to begin with our physical, we might become suicides. And neither the fanatic nor the suicide do any disentangling: on the contrary, they involve themselves more, and most painfully so. The burden of their kamma becomes well-nigh unbearable!

It is as if we had to unwind a ball of twine. There is but one end at which we can start. That portion which has been wound on last totally envelops the more central portions. The entire ball is but one thread which has been wound about itself to such an extent that now it forms a complicated entity of a certain shape and elasticity. As it unwinds its elasticity changes first, its general shape last. Yet the thread, though losing its complexity, remains entire.

Thus it is with the human entity who works out his kamma. Whilst disentangling the skein of existence his mentality remains totally unbroken and becomes more and more clarified, and though retaining his externalization for the time being, his responsiveness essentially changes. But if he breaks the thread—say by destroying his physical externalization—instead of being able to detach himself completely, he must wait until it shall have grown together again, a most tedious and disagreeable process.

The Chain of Relations : How, we may ask, did we get thus entangled in the first instance ? This is an unpractical question with which we need not concern ourselves to any extent. Ultimate beginnings—if ever there were any—have little interest for us. The entanglement exists and must be dealt with.

Buddhist philosophy, however, expounds that there is a chain of twelve links establishing life as we know it. The first of these links is IGNORANCE, or rather "unknowingness" We may imagine that, before we are a definite entity at all, before any complication sets in, before a self has formed, we might say, it is the unknowingness of that which enters upon self-existence that brings this self-existence about. It may be thought of as the first loop in the string of life, at all events as far as we are concerned. But as soon as that loop has taken shape, all its efforts are bent upon retaining self-existence, even though there be as yet no definite self-consciousness. The will to live separately has sprung into existence which, from the later standpoint, was a mistaken step due to ignorance of what that step was leading to. It is the first glimmer of consciousness, a MISPERCEPTION of what would be the wiser thing to do.

The getting into self-existence was the greatest mistake we ever made. Buddhism does not hesitate here: it does not confound issues. Responsibility for subsequent pain and grief is not placed upon the shoulders of a creator, divine or satanic. *We* made the mistake, and ever since we have suffered for it. "What think ye is more," asks the Buddha of his friars, "the tears ye have shed as ye passed from life to life, grieving for the loss of father, mother, sisters, brothers, wives and sweethearts, children and friends, over and over in endless succession, or the waters of the five great oceans?"

However, we are able to rectify our error. Not, indeed, by turning upon our tracks and reversing the process, nor by widening the circle in which we are pursuing ourselves; but rather by gradually narrowing the ring and slowing down until we reach the balancing point, the centre. But of that later.

It was our misperception, our will to self-existence, which brought us SELF-CONSCIOUSNESS, the feeling of what seemed self and what seemed not-self. As soon as that was working there was no end to complications We began to respond to impacts from without, like a man responding to the calling of his name, and as we advanced in RESPONSIVENESS so our form became more complex, more organic. Cells grouped together dividing labour, some to develop responsiveness in one direction, such as to sound waves; others in another direction, such as to light vibrations. The various SENSE ORGANS were developed by responding more and more to the infinite calls for response for that which was not the self to that which had constituted itself as such. CONTACT was established with the world without, and the more we contacted the better we remembered whether that contact was agreeable or not. The subsequent EMOTION of the pleasant and the unpleasant was evoked. The unpleasant we began to avoid as much as possible, and we sought after the pleasant. As the emotions became more complex, our sense of what was pleasant became more fastidious. We desired more, and were less frequently able to satisfy that desire. Thus there arose CRAVING, the thirst for the pleasurable, for that which was attainable with difficulty. And at those times that we did succeed in obtaining what we desired we were loth to let go again, realizing how difficult it would be to find a satisfying substitute for the thing to which we clung with such ATTACHMENT. But as every combination must sooner or later fall back into its constituent elements, whatever we felt attached to had to be relinquished again sooner or later. That did not change our *feeling* of attachment, however; it merely suspended for the time being our realization of that attachment. And it was our very thirst for a renewal of the pleasurable contact, our desire for PERPETUATION, that remained active as a force of suction, of indrawing, causing us to repeat over and over again the realization of connection with the thing sought, of self-identification with the thing found, as well as the loss of that connection and the disillusionment attendant upon attempted self-identification! But knowing no better, we continued to thirst for renewed satisfaction, for wider experience, not realizing that it was as hopeless fully to satisfy our cravings as it is to satisfy one's thirst by drinking water out of the ocean. Thus we established ourselves as a whirlpool of centripetal forces, ever attempting to hold, ever loth to relinquish; ever unable to hold, ever forced to relinquish! As the whirl became more intense, our existence assumed a cyclic measure. We became subject to BIRTH AFTER BIRTH, swirling in ever larger cycles, through more complex forms, with more refined sensations and more delicate responsiveness. And it is thus that we are here, subject to DECREPITUDE AND DEATH, SORROW AND LAMENTATION, EVIL, GRIEF AND DESPAIR!

To sum up this twelve-linked chain of relations, we have:

1. Ignorance.
2. Misperception.
3. Self-consciousness.
4. Responsiveness and shape.
5. Sense organs.

6. Contact.
7. Emotion.
8. Craving.
9. Attachment.
10. Perpetuation.
11. Birth after birth.
12. Decrepitude, death, sorrow, evil, grief and despair.

But it is not necessary to consider this chain historically, as we did above. It holds good contemporaneously equally well. For with regard to any matter whatsoever it is through our ignorance that our perception is warped, that our self-consciousness is affected, that we respond and mould our appearance accordingly, that our sense organs are adjusted, our contact established, our emotions touched, craving evinced, attachment created, that we are perpetuating ourselves as separative entities to be reborn from moment to moment and from lifetime to lifetime in ever greater complexities of sorrow.

However we look upon this chain of relations—whether as affecting our entire self-existence or as touching any single act of entanglement contributory to self-existence—it holds good in its entirety, it has no loop-hole. It is a logical and remorseless statement of fact which only the mature mind can adequately appreciate, even as only strong eyes can glory in the brightness of a midsummer's day!

Cause and Effect: With the foregoing analysis of the twelve-linked chain of existence the subject of kamma is by no means exhausted. In our misappreciation of oriental philosophical concepts due to faulty translations ; to under-estimation of their value ; to a supercilious sense of the superiority of the pale races over the more naturally coloured ones ; to the materialistic view that an industrial and mechanical advancement is of greater human value than a mental and spiritual ; to all these mistaken views—not considering the superstitions with which we are imbued and which we dignify by the name of religion—we must attribute our utter ignorance of and general disregard for the finest products of mentality the human race has so far been able to unfold.

Our views of the laws of cause and effect are as yet exceedingly crude. When we observe that two phenomena invariably occur one subsequent to the other we naturally assume a connection between them. For example when we see a cloudy sky and then see raindrops come we are apt to say that the cloud is the cause of the rain. Then we ask for the cause of the cloud, and then for the cause of that cause, until finally we are logically compelled to assume an illogical First Cause to make the other causes workable ! Now Buddhism is not guilty of any such concept as a First Cause. There never was a First Cause, as there will never be a Last Effect. There are but

*7

sets of circumstance to which our consciousness responds in greater or lesser degree, and in greater or lesser complexity.

Returning to the cloud and the rain in our example, it is quite obvious that there is a connection between the two phenomena, but it is *not* one of cause and effect. The rain is not the effect of the cloud in the sky. Both cloud and rain are part and parcel of the same phenomenon. The cloud *is* the rain to be precipitated. Even as the rain is not caused by the cloud but is a portion of the ensemble of parts and forces bound together as one temporary unit, so when we speak in our crude way about cause and effect, what we really mean is that two separate impressions are made upon our sense of perception by the same set of circumstances, and the further apart in time these impressions are, that is to say the more intermediate impressions are experienced, the more we are lulling ourselves mentally by murmuring the blanket catchwords "cause and effect"! As if that settled the problem!

All phenomena which we are capable of observing, together with many we may not be able to observe, hang together and interact as part and parcel of one larger phenomenon, of which our observations are but partial impressions. That is why we experience them as separate and attribute to them false notions of time and space. Our own sense capacities put together those things that we regard as units. When we speak of a city or a nation or a race, there are not these definite outlines which we must use in order to formulate our thoughts! The boundaries of a city are purely arbitrary and can be changed by proclamation. The units comprising a nation are separate individuals that need have no ethnological interrelations, whilst those belonging to a race may or may not be "pure" stock. So with childhood, youth and manhood. Who can say at what day and hour the one changes into the next? We have a general notion whether a person is a child or a youth or a man, but the periods of transition are indefinable. All things are constantly changing, no thing is the same thing for two consecutive moments. They are all in a state of flux, of motion, of adjustment, of response. It is our mind that creates the outlines, the limitations. We cannot say that the child is the cause of the youth and the youth that of the man. They are interconnected states of the same set of circumstances. We attribute qualities, characteristics, notions to the various parts of the set, and then falsely treat these parts as independent units, calling one the cause of the other!

What there is, then, is not so much cause and effect as interrelation and interaction. The various parts interact, call forth a reaction one from the other. They are there all simultaneously, like the pages in a book or the pictures on a film, but as they appear before our mind's eye so do we see them in succession. Only we are part of the set of film pictures, so to speak, not merely onlookers. We take part in the process of reaction: in fact, it is our reaction which creates our world for us. We have the faculty of controlling our response to certain calls for reaction, both by suppression and by stimulation. Buddhism might be called the Science of Response Control; Buddhist effort is to suppress the undesirable, the grosser responsiveness, and substitute the desirable, the finer, for it. That kind of responsiveness is undesirable which is inextricably interrelated with suffering and pain: we say, for briefness' sake, which causes suffering and pain, though we mean that it is part of that kind of set of circumstances. We have a similar verbal inaccuracy when we speak of the rising and setting of the sun or the moon. Our way of speaking does not deceive any person in the least degree educated. Even so when the Buddhist speaks of cause and effect, it does not deceive any with the least amount of Right Understanding: it is a convenient way of expressing himself in familiar terms. We know that those sets of circumstances of which pain and suffering are parts are those that further entangle us, that are related with desire sensations, with craving and the indulgence of craving. Craving alone produces evil, pain suffering misery. This is the whole secret of Buddhism. Detachment is the keyword to the solution of the problem. Detachment of its own accord leads to disentanglement: not because it is the cause of disentanglement, but because it is part and parcel of that set of circumstances of which disentanglement is one! Detachment is the avoidance of craving!

But if we cannot speak of cause and effect in this way, how is it that we have to wait after one phenomenon for the next one belonging to the same set to take place? Why do they not occur simultaneously? The answer is that we are so constituted that we cannot survey the entire field of experience at one glance. It is like reading a book or travelling a road. The entire road is there though, on account of our peculiar methods of locomotion and our short range of vision, we can only be aware of a small portion of it at one time. But as we travel along, the remainder of the road enters our consciousness, little by little until, when we come to the end, we say we have travelled the road. But our travelling has not been the cause of the road, nor is the portion upon which we happen to find ourselves at any one time the cause of the next portion. Nor even is our travelling the cause of our seeing the road, since we see but a little of it at one time: the one is coincident with the other, not the cause of the other. It is all part and parcel of the same set of circumstances. and we have the option to travel the road quickly or slowly, on foot or on horseback, on a bicycle or in an automobile, to look sideways or forward. The set of circumstances is there: how shall we respond?

Now this same line of reasoning holds good with regard to the twelve-linked chain of relations. Where there is one of the twelve links present, there of necessity must be also the other eleven. This series is often called the Chain of Causation, more as a matter of convenience than as a matter of fact. We may compare it to a wheel with twelve spokes. Only one point of that wheel touches the ground at any one time; but were it not for the remaining portions which *must* follow in due succession, and which support the point supporting the wheel, there could be no wheel, no progression, no motion. And if we break out only one single section of the wheel's circumference, the entire structure falls to pieces. It does not matter where we begin. The entire set is so interrelated that by the removal of one section the remainder automatically collapses.

Again, we may ask how it is that any action on our part must of necessity return to *us*. As a matter of fact, any act—including any thought or feeling—which we perform never really leaves us. It sets going a set of circumstances which revolves about us until all the energy put into it has exhausted itself. We may use another analogy here. Suppose I stand at the centre of a globe and throw a ball in any direction. That ball *must* rebound to me at the centre. Thus it is that any action on my part, whether physical, emotional or mental, produces kamma, that is to say, returns to me. I am throwing actions, thoughts and feelings in all directions : but I am at the centre of a globe of action, so to speak. That globe is of my own sustaining, it has been produced by my energy of craving and as long as there is that sustaining energy so long will that globe remain in existence and so long must it of necessity have a centre. This centre I feel as my I, my Self. But the energy released is as much part of the self as is the centre whence it proceeded. Therefore the whole conformation is my Self, my Kamma. The centre sustains the circumference and the circumference retains the centre, all on account of the energy actually at work between the two. If we cease to add to this energy (and this energy is that produced by craving, thirst, suction) the globe of self will gradually fade out ; that is to say it will cease to exist as soon as the still available energy has exhausted itself. And that will be the end of kamma.

We cannot therefore say that we produce kamma so much as that we *are* kamma maintaining itself, adding unto itself, enlarging itself, entangling itself. Ceasing to crave and to hold and to be attached is equivalent to ceasing to make further kamma and to putting an end to already existing kamma. And when existing kamma has become exhausted and no new kamma engendered, there is an end to all suffering, to all misery actual and potential, and Nibbana will have been attained.

Thus we must understand this self of ours as a reactive principle which, for its very existence, requires the exercise of constant adaptation. This self is kamma, this exercise is kamma. If the adaptation can be made without undue strain, the kamma involved is pleasant. If there is a strain involved—either because there is over-adaptation or under-adaptation—the kamma is unpleasant and even painful. We can place ourselves in one of three positions :

1. That in which a reaction is called for that cannot be taken care of by the organism, such as holding a finger in boiling water: inevitably producing kamma that is painful.

2. That in which a reaction is called for that can well be taken care of by the organism, such as holding a finger in warm water: producing kamma that is pleasurable.

3. That in which no reaction is called for because there is immediate and complete adaptation: being productive of no kamma at all. This last condition may, in a certain sense, be compared to dipping one's finger in water of the same temperature as the finger, calling forth no temperature reaction and thus being unnoticeable in that respect.

It is wise, therefore, to make ourselves so utterly adaptable, physically, emotionally and mentally that, without attachment, without craving, we shall be able immediately to respond to any circumstances that may present themselves to the consciousness, at the same time raising the consciousness to such a level that it will refuse to react at all to those sets of circumstances that are inherently undesirable. Buddhism provides us with a training making it possible for us to attain to such a state. Before discussing this, however, we must turn to the make-up of man, to the five aggregates or khandhas, in order to have a better conception of the complex which constitutes our self and to penetrate into the nature of what we call I.

THE FIVE CONSTITUENTS

THE five constituents or khandhas that go to make a human individual may be enumerated as follows:

1. Bodiliness or form;
2. Sensation;
3. Perception;
4. The Tendencies;
5. Awareness.

Although theoretically we can deal with each of these khandhas separately, in reality it is as difficult actually to isolate any of these five as is the proverbial unscrambling of eggs! They are so dependent each upon the others that were we even theoretically to withdraw a single khandha from the fivefold group, the remaining four would form an untenable combination. They could not be conceived as a reality any more than could a sheet of paper without thickness or a square without angles.

But since our mind can act synthetically only after having considered a subject analytically, we must deal with the khandhas one by one, after which it will be more easy to grasp them as a combination, even as in endeavouring to understand the geography of any particular region, instead of drawing a map embodying all possible geographical features, we draw for convenience sake several outlines of the same region and fill in one say with mountains, rivers and wooded sections; another with cities, railways and telegraph communications; another with indications as to the geological conformation and contents of that particular region; still another one showing atmospheric conditions, etc. In every case, however, we know that the map we are consulting but partially represents the description of the region we are investigating. Thus it is with the khandhas. Each one constitutes a response capacity in the region of the human self covering a different field; none deals with the self as a whole; each one with an essential aspect of the self; all five together with every feature constituting the human entity.

The khandhas generally are enumerated in the order in which they logically attract our attention. When we awaken mentally we begin to look about us, and as our minds get adjusted to the reality of things, having discarded or holding in abeyance all previously conceived notions and theories, we take things in the order of their incidence and interpret them to the best of our ability. As this process proceeds, adjustments are necessary here and there, just as, when awakening from deep and dreamful sleep, we gradually make adjustments concerning the nature of the things we observe. An apparent shadow may become an object, an object a shadow, a streak of light becomes a brass bed rail or a window, a splash of colour on the wall resolves itself into an ornamental flower design. Our dream theories are discarded: we are awake!

Thus it is when we awaken to the Buddha thought. Let us discard, or at least hold in abeyance, our religious, philosophical and scientific theories for the time being. Let us begin to observe with a mind awakened. Then, after having opened our mental eyes to the world about us, let us proceed to make the necessary adjustments, after which it is time enough to remember our preconceived notions and accept or discard whatever seems fit.

So in considering the khandhas, let us open our mental eyes and observe.

Bodiliness or Form: The first thing that strikes us in considering any object is the impression it makes upon our senses, more particularly upon our sense of sight. When anything strikes our vision the shade or colour strikes first, which then resolves itself into form or a combination of forms. Thus we attribute to every object with which we come into touch, first colour or shade and then form or shape. We might even go so far as to leave out form altogether since it is only by contrast between shades that form is visually recognized. However, we have become so accustomed to deal with things in their shapes rather than in their colours, that as a rule we lay more stress on that secondary quality of objects than on the primary.

Amongst all the forms which surround us as objects within the purview of our senses the human form to us is of course the most important, and that for two reasons : firstly, because we recognize ourselves as endowed with it ; secondly, because it serves as a standard of comparison for all other forms of which we become aware.

There is only one fundamental factor involved in our visual recognition of either shade or shape, and that is contrast. Where there is no contrast there is no basis for comparison, for there is no noticeable difference. If all things had exactly the same colour, if they were all, say, sky-blue of exactly the same hue and the same luminosity, we would not only be unconscious of the fact that the sky was blue, but we would also be utterly unaware that there was anything at all. There would be neither colour nor outline ; neither shade nor shape ; and our eye consciousness would immediately cease to be operative. It is contrast, therefore, which is the basis of both colour and shape.

It may be objected here that though we respond to colour by means of our sense of sight, it is our sense of touch which brings us into contact with form. If we live, as many human beings do live, without the sense of sight, we are still aware that things have shape, though we do not assign to them any particular shade. Although this is quite true, we must not forget that, when we enumerate the various senses, namely: sight, touch, hearing, smell, and taste, we may regard each one of them as a variation of any of the other four. We might say, for example, that touch is seeing in the realm of contact ; hearing is seeing in the realm of sound ; and even that smelling and tasting are particular kinds of seeing. We refer all things touched or heard or tasted or smelled to visual memory, and this holds good more particularly to things touched because the shape suggested by the touch has to be constructed by a kind of inner vision, has to be visualized ! The aim of any one of the senses is merely to get into a particular kind of touch with things about us, to respond in a specific way. Says the Buddha, in reference to the senses : "These five senses, Brother, have different fields, different ranges ; they do not share each other's field and range. Of them, thus mutually independent, the mind is their resort, and the mind partakes of, enjoys the field and range of them all."

Nor are colour and form exactly confined to the senses of sight and touch. This we recognize in popular language when we speak of the form of a poem or of a composition, or of the colour of a musical theme, thus referring the same faculties to our sense of hearing. The reason that we do not do the same with our senses of taste and smell is probably because they are habitually of more utilitarian and less æsthetic use : though who shall say whether a dog does not visualize his smell perceptions in terms of form or colour ?

Again, when speaking of the bodiliness of objects we do not merely refer to their physical form and their physical colour. If it is maintained that there are superphysical colours and shapes, there is no reason why the first khandha should not be applied to such colours and shapes also. Wherever there is bodiliness and wherever there is the suggestion of shape, by whatever senses they are brought into the consciousness of the observer, there the first khandha is operative. "All form whatsoever, O Monks, whether past, future, or present, whether subjective or objective, gross or subtile, low or exalted, near or distant, pertains to the form-group," says the Buddha.

The first khandha, therefore, comprising bodiliness and appearance, combined or separate, as applied to the self of man, reaches from the coarsest portions of the physical vehicle to the most tenuous effusions of the most refined parts of his constitution.

It is thus clearly to be understood that in so far as bodiliness plays a part in the active expression of man's selfhood, there the first khandha exists. And when it is maintained that "even thoughts have forms," that "even emotions have colours," the forms of the thoughts and the colours of the emotions in their own regions represent the first khandha.

Sensation: The second khandha or constituent of the self is sensation. That is to say, whenever one of the senses is affected so that a change occurs in its adjustment, there a sensation takes place and there the second khandha is at work. It does not matter whether the sensation is vague or defined, whether it is mild or intense: whenever the eye is affected by sheen or by shadow, the ear by sound or by silence, the touch and the smell and the taste in their own particular ways; and where, in consequence, we are affected so as to receive a noticeable impression, there we have sensation. Whether it is our physical senses or any other senses that are thus affected: wherever it is, the second khandha operates. "All sensation whatsoever, O Monks, whether past, future, or present, whether subjective or objective, gross or subtile, low or exalted, near or distant, pertains to the sensation group," says the Buddha.

Now it matters little what really it is that so affects our senses as to leave an impress. Whatever may be the nature of what is outside of us, to us it becomes reality only in so far as we associate sensations with it. The impacts connected with sensation are separate, but follow so closely one upon the other that they are felt as continuous.

We speak of them as vibrations, a term happily coined, it being indicative both of the momentary and oscillatory nature and the continuous flux of what are to us such important realities. All that we call matter, substance, is what reaches us through our sensations. When we speak of matter that does not reach us in this way directly, such as superphysical substance, we refer to a concept that reaches our understanding through sympathetic sensations, for in such a case we must first think of substance that we can sense, physical substance, then subtract the physical and substitute for it the superphysical. It reaches us through our sensations indirectly.

As to the actual constitution of matter, as far as we are concerned it may have none, and we may even agree with those western philosophers who maintain that it is not substance so much as a complex of qualities that impinges upon our senses. Nor need we seek for an actual substratum underlying these qualities. Whether there is such a substratum or not it is of little value for us to consider, since it is the qualities only of matter—colour, weight, size, shape, and the like—that enter our consciousness and that constitute what wo torm reality. The moment we experience a sensation we touch what to us is a reality, and in so far as it *is* a reality to us we feel pleasantly, unpleasantly, or indifferently affected. Our senses go out and grapple with what they find. Their mission is to arrest the oscillatory movement, the perpetual flux, long enough to turn it into definite and stable outlines to be submitted to us for our examination, like a dog rapporting a stone or a child grabbing a handful of earth from a sandheap and holding it up for inspection. That our senses do not for a single moment arrest the flux outside need not be emphasized, but it must be remembered that their task is fulfilled when they succeed in retaining a definite impression of some sort long enough to be turned over to the consciousness as something stable and fixed, just like a photographer succeeds in getting the picture of a diver apparently poised in mid-air, head downwards, when in reality he is in the course of falling between the diving board and the water. In other words, nothing is in a state of being; all is in a condition of "becoming—other"

It is indeed difficult so clearly to indicate the limitation of one khandha without encroaching upon the territory of the next, that a separate mental picture can be had of its particular sphere of operation. The khandhas overlap into each other's territory even as the gray of a cloud merges into the white, and the more closely we endeavour to analyze the khandhas the less definite become their individual outlines, just as the closer we approach the cloud the more hazy do become its features.

It is thus that any sensation associated with the adjustment of our senses to outline and bodiliness inevitably gives rise to the third khandha, perception.

Perception: This third constituent, perception, may be regarded as the sounding-board behind sensation. No object can be perceived except through the sensation it imparts, and although this is a truism, in considering the khandhas it is to be postulated as a special function in the combination.

The point where a sensation turns into a perception is also the point where a vague general pervasion is transformed into a clear and definite entity, even as the light of the sun caught by a lens is concentrated into a distinct and perceptible picture. It is the point where feeling changes into mentality; where an impression leaves an imprint; where general being becomes a particular self. A perception may be regarded as the crystallization of a sensation. Whereas the sensation does not go further than our feelings, perception reaches our mental structure. The mind cannot work without perception. Its very basis is perception, even as perception relies on sensation, and even as sensation is dependent upon bodiliness and outline. Through whichever particular senses perception affects the mind, whether those senses be physical or superphysical, the third khandha is operative. "All perception whatsoever, O Monks, whether past, future, or present, whether subjective or objective, gross or subtile, low or exalted, near or distant, pertains to the perception-group," says the Buddha.

It must not be assumed, however, that immediately a sensation turns into a perception, the perception is necessarily a correct one. It is only after prolonged experience that the perception evoked becomes definite enough to be fitted around and connected with the already existing concepts in the mind and falls into its proper place there. As long as it is wild, that is to say as long as the percept remains unconnected, it cannot become, or merge with, a concept. Finding no fitting place in the mental structure, it gives rise to no understanding. But as soon as it attaches itself to an already present concept or finds a niche of its own, we say that we understand the thing. A concept, then, is a percept or group of percepts upon which the entity relies for its reaction.

The Tendencies: The complexity of this fourth khandha is more apparent than real. By the tendencies is meant the reaction incident upon perception. As soon as I perceive an object by becoming aware of the sensations induced by its bodiliness and outline, there immediately a reaction is called forth which depends altogether upon the contents of the mind at the moment the perception takes place.

Suppose I see a chair. First my eye is affected by the shade and the shape of the object. This produces a sensation, the sensation is translated into a perception, and the perception calls forth a tendency with regard to the chair. If I am standing and am tired, it will produce a desire to sit down upon the chair. If the chair belongs to another person and is handsomer than any I have, it may call forth a wish to possess it. If it is a rickety old chair and I am a fat old man, I may feel tempted to use it preferably for fire wood At any rate, as soon as I perceive an object, there is a tendency to react upon my perception in a way conditioned by my experience with reference to similar perceptions in the past.

The fourth khandha, then, comprises all tendencies to reaction, such as desire, will, inclination, attraction, repulsion, and many others. Here again it must be emphasized that the fourth khandha is so bound up with the other khandhas that it is hardly possible to set it up separately, but it comprises the entire reactive machinery of the mind, and that not merely as a simple progression, but as a complex one, bent in upon itself, so to speak. Like a mirror bent double, reflecting itself within itself infinitely in either direction and reflecting any object held between the surfaces infinitely in either direction, so the mind—a similarly reflective medium—as soon as it perceives, will reflect the perception within itself into infinitude. Suppose I perceive a tree; I may perceive that I perceive a tree; I may perceive that I perceive that I perceive a tree, etc. The tendency to react upon any perception, therefore, may be almost literally said to be due to the bent of the mind. Even as a tree bends to the wind, so the mind bends to the impact of forms, of sensations, and of percepts, according to its own elastic responsiveness.

In this fourth khandha, then, we have the responsive capacity in all its phases. To enumerate all these is as futile a procedure as to recite all the numerals or to classify all possible letter combinations. We know them on account of the principle involved which is the reactive principle, and it is hardly worth while to make an attempt at expressing every possible reaction that can be called forth from out of the constituent elements of the human self! "All tendencies whatsoever, O Monks, whether past, future, or present, whether subjective or objective, gross or subtile, low or exalted, near or distant, pertain to the tendencies-group," says the Buddha.

It must not be overlooked, of course, that there is a great difference between the reactive capacity of different human beings and although this does not in any way affect the principle involved, it greatly affects the individual expression of each entity: in other words, it establishes identity. We may even say that the chief difference between one human being and another lies in his reactive faculties ; in his capacity to respond, and in his control over the exercise of this capacity.

The tendencies with which each human being reacts are based upon the entire contents of his consciousness, including the latest perception. What is meant by the contents of his consciousness ? To reply to this question we are logically driven to consider the fifth khandha, that of consciousness or awareness.

Awareness : Even as each one of the constituents pervades and is associated with the other four, so the khandha of awareness pervades and is inextricably bound up with bodiliness and appearance, sensation, perception, and the reactive tendencies. "All consciousness whatsoever, O Monks, whether past, future, or present, whether subjective or objective, gross or subtle, low or exalted, near or distant, pertains to the consciousness-group."

The principle underlying awareness is focus or adjustment. My eyes see an object only so long as a certain period of adjustment is not exceeded. My mind grasps a concept only so long as its focussing power does not lose its elasticity. If I stare at an article before me on my desk I shall cease to see it after a short while, because by not moving the eye muscles and by not further having to adjust the lens of the eye the visual apparatus becomes totally adjusted, whereupon the object ceases to impinge upon the consciousness. The only method whereby it can be seen once more is by turning the eye in another direction so as to change the focus of the lens, and then turning it back on to the object, thus changing the focus once more; or else by moving the object itself, which serves the same end. In either case I am calling for a new adjustment. But if I keep the eye inactive, and the object immovable, its shade and shape will gradually disappear and will be obliterated entirely as soon as the sight mechanism has completely consented to be at rest.

Exactly similar is the process of sensation. Sensation becomes inhibited when the mechanism has ceased to be in a state of potential adjustment to the thing to be sensed. If I touch the object before me, I shall be aware of my touch sensation as long as the tactile nerves are responding to the impact of the object. If I hold my fingers still and relaxed upon the same spot, it will be but a little while before I shall be entirely unable to be aware of my touch sensation.

The perception, being dependent upon the sensation, must cease with the latter, and the reactive tendencies must naturally follow suit and cease to be reactive. True, I still may have the memory of the sensation, which may act as a new sensation, the overtone of the original one, so to speak, inducing a new state of consciousness. Or I may retain the memory of the perception which, acting as a new perception, calls forth a new response tendency and may induce a new state of consciousness. Or again, a response may be repeated from memory, thus inducing a new state of consciousness. But in all such cases the memory or repetition of either the sensation, the perception, or the response thereto acts just as does a new sensation, perception, or response.

The memory or recurrence of a sensation, a perception, a response tendency, is in the nature of a reflex, and is akin to the reappearance on the eye retina of a light impression after the original picture has disappeared. The reason for the long time periods that may intervene between any of these mental recurrences as compared to those on the eye retina lies in the fact that the media with which they are concerned are so much more plastic, retentive, and elastic. That we can recall such memories at will, and that they are subject to our control, is due to the very nature of the will which, being one of the response tendencies, can be appealed to, and can set the entire human machinery in motion. But that holds good for any of the five constituents or any of their aspects or combinations, as long as the machinery is unimpaired and as long as the connections are not broken or interfered with. It is like setting in motion a wheel: upon whichever portion of the wheel we exercise pressure, the entire wheel will be made to turn in accordance with the amount and the direction of the pressure exercised.

Now just as there is an eye retina for the registering of shades, so is there a retina on which the sensations, one on which the perceptions, and one on which the response tendencies are being registered. It is the consciousness, in fact, which constitutes these retinæ, which is their general confluence ; for it is the very consciousness which holds, which retains, and from which can be recalled previous impressions. A process of reflection goes on unintermittently between these various retinæ or centres of consciousness. And although the mechanism as such works automatically, we gradually acquire more and more control over our response tendencies which we learn to inhibit whenever their full play is seen to give rise to suffering, or to stimulate if the occasion so demands ; just as we can refrain from stealing once we understand that it is not conducive to well-being, or can stretch forth our hand to receive a proffered gift.

Thus shade and shape are reflected within the sensations ; the sensations by the perceptions ; the perceptions through the tendencies. Each of these constituents can be retranslated into the terms of its origin : the tendencies into perceptions ; the perceptions into sensations ; the sensations into forms. These processes of reflection, going on without cessation, intermingling and intermixing, constitute our existence, our being, our very self!

Our consciousness, therefore, may be appropriately classified according to the other four constituents, and in this manner we obtain four kinds of awareness:

(1) consciousness of bodiliness or form;
(2) consciousness of sensation;
(3) consciousness of perception;
(4) consciousness of tendencies; all of which may intermingle in various proportions.

Now as to consciousness itself. It is often assumed that consciousness is something outside of substance, that it is superimposed upon substance, that consciousness as such exists in a region all its own—the region of the All-Consciousness—whence it condescends to be drawn down to the regions of matter which it penetrates and permeates and where it manifests in various degrees according to the nature of the instrument at its disposal. According to this theory consciousness is but dimly present in the mineral kingdom, becomes somewhat more definite in the vegetable region, is quite in evidence in the animal world, and reaches its climax, at least in so far as this physical existence is concerned, in humankind. There are philosophies which continue this process through still higher kingdoms, those of the angels, archangels, principalities, powers, virtues, dominions, thrones, cherubim and seraphim, up to the very Godhead, but the principle upon which their idea is based varies in no respect from that enunciated, and which consists in assuming that Consciousness as such will manifest wherever it has the opportunity of doing so, just as light shines through a window, and that the reason why it is dimmer in the kingdoms below the human than it is in the higher kingdoms is because in the former it has not as translucent an instrument through which to work, on the same principle that the light of the sun can penetrate a clear and clean glass better than it can a dim and dirty one.

The theory just referred to has found favour with not a few modern thinkers, in spite of the fact that its chief inconsistency lies in that it postulates Consciousness as one thing, Matter as another and an utterly different thing, yet proposing a relation between the two!

From the Buddhist point of view the theory in point does not hold water, and is on a par with the dogma of an ultimate, all-knowing, omnipotent, and perfect Deity ruling over a very imperfect world of his own creating; with only the word Consciousness substituted for Godhead!

The problem of consciousness as a Buddhist concept is much more simple than the same problem as viewed by any other philosophy.

We have already seen that life and substance are inseparable, that there is neither life without substance nor substance without life. It is easy to recognize that a tree, for example, is living. That a table made out of a tree is also living, however, is a little more difficult to understand. But it is obvious that the live wood of which the table is made retains its life as long as it is in existence, and should the table be broken to pieces, the chips still retain the life of the wood. Should it be burned, then, truly, as wood it is no longer living, but the ash particles retain a vitality of their own which is evident from the fact that we find them suitable for fertilizing purposes, when their life is absorbed by the growing plant. There is, then, no substance that has no life, in fact, that is not life itself, though it need not be organized substance to which we refer.

Now exactly the same condition holds good with regard to consciousness. Consciousness, says the Buddhist, is the very essence of substance; nor can there be any substance without consciousness at any time under any circumstances. It is as necessary an attribute of matter as is life, and neither matter nor consciousness can exist or be thought of the one independently of the other. Wherever matter exists, there consciousness is to be found; wherever there is consciousness, there substance of some sort must be in evidence.

Now the question may be asked: "If all substance has consciousness as an attribute, is a table or a house conscious also?" To which we reply that, though in reality the substance of which the table or the house is made is indeed quite as conscious as the same substance elsewhere, there is no consciousness on the part of the wood in the table or the masonry in the house as to the fact that it has been made into a table or combined into a house. The division of labour in the wood particles holds good only in so far as they formed the tree and partook in the tree's organization. But when the tree is cut down and sawed into planks out of which a table has been manufactured, though the particles composing the wood do not lose any of their consciousness, in so far as their labour had been divided to serve the purposes of the tree and not those of the table, they continue to be tree-conscious, if we may use such an expression, until decay sets in and they are released from their collective task.

Although in our explanation we have referred mainly to matter physical, we do not by any means exclude so-called superphysical substance. In fact, from our point of view the only difference between the two is that the average human senses are adjusted to certain grades of substance which for that reason we call "physical"—though perhaps a better word would be "noticeable"—and that substance to which they are not attuned or responsive—the "unnoticeable"—we refer to as superphysical. But even the finest degree of substance imaginable, even that through which our thoughts and our emotions and our subtlest functions operate, even that which is generally viewed as unsubstantial and purely spiritual, is regarded as substance with its corresponding attribute of consciousness. So that we may say that, if there is consciousness everywhere, it is because there is substance of some sort everywhere, and *vice-versa.*

In order adequately to account for the facts of existence, however, an additional explanation has to be made. The consciousness with which we are dealing is not pure substance-consciousness: that we can as little postulate as pure substance itself. No final matter-unit is thinkable, since each unit to which we trace back constitutes a complex having finer units of its own, each of which in turn comprises still finer units. The same argument holds good for the life attribute and for the consciousness attribute of matter, so that the word matter in the Buddhist sense means something entirely different from the same word used colloquially. When we speak of matter we combine such ideas as perceptibility (even though but mental), life, consciousness, retentiveness, activity, cohesiveness and other tendencies. Matter, instead of being one of the simplest mental concepts, becomes one of the most complex ones.

Here the question might be asked: "If matter has all those qualities usually ascribed to a perfect Godhead, is not this system a kind of materialism with the word 'Matter' substituted for 'Deity'?" To which we reply: "Not so, for the idea of a Godhead postulates these qualities in their perfection and purity, entirely abstracted from substance which is employed for the purpose of showing them forth; whereas in our conception there is no such thing as a final unit of matter, for as we drive our conception of things backward to the next lower unit—say the atom—or forward to the next higher—say the solar system—in either case we have to deal with a complex of the next lower or higher grade respectively. Just as we can conceive no final material atom, so we can conceive no final spiritual creator."

Now when similar units of consciousness come together, cling together, they tend to combine to form a new unit of a higher order, that is to say they tend to divide labour amongst themselves, thus working towards organization. Separate organs are formed to take care of specific functions. In so far as that organ is concerned, there is unit-form, there is unit-sensation, there is unit-perception, there is unit-responsiveness, there is unit-consciousness: in fine, the five khandhas or constituents are present. We cannot get away from the Five Constituents!

Again, wherever there is a complete sub-unit composed of the five khandhas, there we have a sub-retina of consciousness. An example is afforded by the eye which will close itself upon the approach of an insect or a dust particle before the fact penetrates to our mental consciousness. The sub-unit in charge of the eye organism, so to speak, will respond of its own accord even before communicating with the general retina of consciousness, the self-consciousness, and will make such adjustments as are momentarily required. There are similar sub-retinæ for our digestive system, our nervous system, our emotional nature, our mentality, etc., some of which have become entirely sub-conscious, some partly so, meaning that the greater consciousness of the entire human organism only becomes affected when any particular sub-conscious centre stands before an impasse which requires an unfamiliar response.

Wherever there is impact there is a call for response. In such response several particles collectively participate, and by so clinging together—we might almost say for self-protection—they tend to form an organism to withstand and respond in its entirety, as a newly formed unit, to the impacts from without, for the purpose of adjusting itself thereto. The organism comes into being through division of response-labour amongst the various particles constituting it. By thus endeavouring to respond and withstand the outside impact and to become adjusted thereto, friction is engendered amongst the particles, that is to say kamma, thus establishing knowledge of response, or self-consciousness. In such manner a new unit of consciousness results, with its own retina, together with its inseparable kamma.

Like the other constituents, therefore, the khandha of consciousness is a response mechanism which, on account of its slow and inadequate adjustment, becomes conscious of itself as a whole. The slowness of its adjustment is due to the division of labour amongst the constituent particles—which itself is evidence of their inherent consciousness—and to the internecine friction whenever a response is called for by an impact from without.

The Social Consciousness: The more highly organized becomes the division of labour, the more highly individual is the resulting entity, and the more definite is the expression of the unit-consciousness. In the case of the human being we have a division of labour, an organization, so complex and so perfect that all the essential requirements of the physical organism are satisfiable. Our heart action, our digestion, our blood circulation, need not any further be consciously regulated. To such activities the entity as a self need no further pay attention and for this reason they have become automatic, and consequently sub-conscious. That is to say that for those activities a retina of consciousness has established itself which takes care of these functions, and it is only when their regular course of action has become interrupted, as when the digestion has become impaired, the heart beats irregularly, or the blood circulates poorly, that the reliance of the self-unit upon that particular action is lessened and the self-consciousness is once more adverted to it. But under normal conditions the attention of the self-consciousness is now being directed towards the formation of a higher unit of organization, a social unit, of which progressive evidence is supplied in the shape of the family, the tribe or the race, the nation, and finally organized internationalism. We may say, therefore, that the destiny of the human race is to become one great organic social unit, in which every nation is to represent an organ and have its specific function to perform, and in which every human being is to constitute say a molecule. It is true that, as this ideal nears achievement, the human units concerned also outgrow the requirements of the human kingdom, making ready to enter the kingdom next above, that of the devas or angels. But meanwhile the social consciousness increases as the personal declines.

This tendency on the part of the human race as a whole to form a social organization is entirely on a par with the tendency on the part of a collection of particles to form an organism within say a human body in the course of formation. Since the human being has become a more or less completed unit it is but natural for a number of such units to join and to divide labour, responding collectively to such external impacts as will affect them as a whole, one portion responding to one kind of impact, another to another kind. Thus the human race is moving in the direction of a social organization, which simply means that it is developing race-consciousness, a self-consciousness of a higher order, of which the brotherhood of man is the keynote, even as in the formation of the human organization of the single entity the co-operative brotherhood of the lower unit particles was the keynote. These processes of integration are repeated from magnitude to magnitude.

It is in the pursuit of this social destiny that the physical functions become subordinate to the emotional and mental ones. For with the increase of social relationships the emotions and the thoughts of the individual also become more and more organized, and the more automatic the bodily activities become, the wider becomes the scope of the emotional and mental possibilities. These in their turn will gradually become more habitual and responsive and, after many human births, ultimately automatic. Thereupon a still higher unit of consciousness will be attained and we shall cease to belong to the human kingdom, advancing to the kingdom beyond. There again, the self-same processes will repeat themselves : the bodily adjustments are made, and subsequently the higher ones; after which comes the next series of births or manifestations, and so on. There is no end to this chain of existences, unless indeed we decide to make the effort required to attain Nibbana at any particular stage.

Nor must we think of this development in the human race of race-consciousness as a positive evolutionary advancement. All previous human races have gone the same way, and upon their shifting from the human region to the one next above, another human race, shifting from the kingdom next below, took its place. And so it will continue. Humanity follows humanity as wave follows wave upon the mighty ocean of progression, the end of which is not. Each wave, therefore, relatively holds its place notwithstanding its progressive motion, even as would a movable centre of a circle whose circumference was infinite. Thus upon the question whether there is such a thing as evolutionary progress we can reply neither with a whole-hearted "Yes," nor with a full-throated "No," just as we could not say whether or not the child and the man into which it grew were one and the same person.

Summary: In recapitulating this chapter we must set forth once more: That the five constituents can be separated only theoretically, but that practically they are bound up together in such a way that it is as impossible to regard them singly as it is "for a man to taste the water of the Bay of Bengal and tell which drop came out of this river and which drop came out of that river". That bodiliness or form are what our senses bring to us each from their own field of action; that we transform these sensations into perceptions to which we respond according to the previous contents of our minds, and that we are aware of all these processes by very virtue of our organization. That this entire organization constitutes our self, our soul, if you like, and that we must guard against "the delusion of supposing that any one of these five constituents either (1) is the soul, as a flame and its colour may be considered one; or (2) is an attribute of soul, as its shadow is an attribute of the tree; or (3) is in the soul, as the perfume is in the flower; or (4) contains the soul, as a casket contains a jewel". Not that we say there is no soul, but we emphatically affirm that there is no such thing as an immutable, non-substantial, eternal soul-entity, existing independently and outside of the five constituents, but that in fact it is the five constituents that constitute the entity in its entirety, soul and body, changing from moment to moment, referring the lower to the higher, though even the highest attribute of our nature in its own region is as much subject relatively to change as is the lowest. That we are concerned neither with the ultimate nature of matter nor with the ultimate nature of spirit, for neither of these extremes is thinkable. That consciousness is an inalienable attribute of substance, as is self-consciousness of organized substance. That a composite entity like the human being has a general self-consciousness which is the confluence of numerous subservient self-consciousnesses which together form our sub-conscious self and each of which is in charge of its own field of activity on account of the division of labour among the units composing the entity. That the human entity in its turn is in the process of coalescing with its fellow human entities, ultimately to constitute a unit in a general race consciousness ; and that by the time this shall have been accomplished, the units composing the present human race will be well on their way towards the next kingdom in the general hierarchy of being, another set of human units, coming up from below taking their place. And that the only way in which to sidestep this eternal progression is to endeavour to tread the Noble Eightfold Path and to make the effort required for the attainment of Nibbana.

NIBBANA

WE now come to the most difficult of all the concepts pertaining to the philosophy of Buddhism, namely that of Nibbana. The difficulty of its comprehension is enhanced by reason of the fact that ever since the subject of Nibbana was brought forward by the early translators of Buddhist writings there has been a great deal of guess work concerning its exact meaning, much to the confusion of the students of the subject. Not only, therefore, must we clear up existing misunderstandings, but we must substitute for them a clear and concise statement of its true meaning, a matter of no little difficulty, as its full significance, of course, can only properly be appreciated by those who have attained this state, just as the description of an automobile or of a locomotive can only draw forth a more or less correct picture in the minds of those who are already acquainted with such vehicles and for whom, therefore, such a description is no longer necessary.

The Futility of Evolution : Now it is only when the futility of the drama of life begins to dawn upon us—when we discover that life in all its bearings is the outcome of past suffering and the harbinger of future distress—that we are ready to consider the problem of Nibbana to practical advantage. If we do not grant the fundamental principle of the prevalence of suffering, we may as well postpone considering this subject until we do. Nor do we mean the distress attendant upon life on earth only, but also the futility of longer periods of heavenly delight which may alternate with and to some extent offset our earth existences if our kamma be such as to bring them about. Craving for life "in heaven"—a clear token that we are disappointed with life here—is as little conducive to the peace of Nibbana as is the desire for life in this earthly sphere.

This sense of futility, then, must reach far beyond mere human existence. During the period intermediate between two earth existences we may be inhabiting realms celestial. Or we might leave the human kingdom altogether and advance to where such celestial spheres become our natural habitat. This, however, involves no promise of *eternal* happiness. It merely means that for the time being the stress of existence has somewhat abated, inducing a sense of relief akin to that of a man just recovered from severe illness. Just as to the latter at first, through the memory of the former period of restraint, the new health condition is a veritable heaven, yet gradually, as that memory fades, he will cease to be so well satisfied ; so the person who has advanced a stage beyond the human kingdom and feels that now, at last, he has reached a condition of bliss and of freedom, will soon discover that even here many things could be changed and improved, are to be suffered and considered, and that there are higher regions still in which the particular disabilities under which he is now labouring do not exist. This constitutes an incentive for him to aspire still higher, until he reaches the stage next beyond, first with relief, gradually with a clearer vision of its disadvantages ; whereupon he again tries to rise higher. This process continues indefinitely, although he may not realize its indefiniteness. It is Buddhism that declares and lays stress upon the futility of such evolutionary progression and proclaims that it is not a necessary path to be followed, that there *is* a way out of the woods, that it is possible and most advisable to sidestep this interminable Jacob's ladder. The Buddha teaches the Existence of Nibbana and the Way Thereto !

Misconceptions Concerning Nibbana: A great many misconceptions exist in the West as in the Orient concerning the nature of Nibbana. Those prevailing in Western countries are chiefly due to the misunderstanding by early translators of Buddhist terms and sentiments. We still have to be very careful in accepting as correct renderings the words and phrases substituted in our inadequate and oftentimes erroneous way for the terms employed in the language of the original. In many cases we possess no equivalents, as in those of samma, dhamma, and kamma ; in other cases the meaning of a word, though correctly rendered, is twisted out of its native shape by different associations and background, as in those of heaven, hell, and God.

It is a very unfortunate circumstance that our theological conceptions have been so largely moulded upon Semitic bombast which has a tendency either to bind us or, in the event that we do manage to break away, to disparage other ideas which we can only express in similar words. Hence the difficulty of presenting Buddhist conceptions to a Western audience who insist upon adding the childish concept of infinity to all their conceptions of the herebefore and the hereafter. Unless we dispense with the "infinite," we cannot enter into the Buddhist cosmology.

The misconception most prevalent in the West regarding Nibbana is that its attainment is equivalent to annihilation, that it is a reduction to nothingness. The Buddha, being questioned upon that point by an inquirer into his doctrine, emphatically declared that he who regards Nibbana as equivalent to annihilation altogether misunderstands the nature and purport of His Teaching. Moreover, one of the ways in which Nibbana is frequently referred to in the Buddhist scriptures is "Amata," meaning "Where there is no more death" or "The Deathless". We need not, therefore, inquire further along this line of thinking since it has been ruled out of court by the Founder of Buddhism Himself.

Nor does "the dewdrop slip into the shiny sea" when Nibbana is attained. No merging with the Absolute is indicated and that for two patent reasons. Firstly, because the Buddhist does not recognize any Absolute; and secondly because such merging, instead of taking him away from the troubles and tribulations attendant upon manifest existence, would only make him participate in the totality of it, thus precipitating him from the frying pan of individual struggle into the fire of universal woe. This is the very thing which the aspirant to Nibbana aims to avoid. He knows full well the possibility of merging his individuality, if not with a universal self, at any rate with that Greater Self whose consciousness pervades a minor universe, say our solar system, and "in whom we live and move and have our being" But he also realizes that, if he pursues that path, though he may immensely prolong his conscious existence, he will undoubtedly take conscious part in the pain and misery as well as in the joy and happiness that pervades the whole of that system, all of which not only is harder to bear but also has not brought him a single step nearer final emancipation. He wisely leaves the joy of creating and the misery of conciliating the creation to the gods and refuses any longer to have a finger in the pie of manifest existence. For the very sake of the world at large he wants to withdraw from it and from all that contributes toward its maintenance. If he aids it onward, even with the best and most unselfish intentions imaginable, he still identifies himself with its struggles, its temporary successes and failures; and though his efforts will undoubtedly bring him the rewards associated with wider consciousness and greater capacities along the same directions, together with a larger sphere wherein to exhaust his energies, at the same time he also entangles himself more and more and accentuates his selfness. True, in so doing he may ultimately reach a place in the vanguard of humanity, excel human nature, and begin to participate consciously in the life of the Deity. He is on the road to godhood, and may become a Deity in his turn, able in time to take charge of a world system of his own. But in this way the process of creation, of reproduction, goes on indefinitely. Relatively speaking, he is not a whit further than he was at the outset of his endeavours: he is still where he was before!

If the Buddha had meant this to be the equivalent to Nibbana, surely there would have been no need for Him to have proclaimed His Message, as the possibility of yoga, of at-one-ment, of unification, of coalescence with the Deity, was already recognized as attainable by every religious system on earth, more particularly by the religion of those amongst whom he sought his first followers! Nibbana is *not*, then, at-one-ment of the human individual with a Deity, a conduction to allness; and this must be most thoroughly emphasized.

Nor is Nibbana a particular heavenly state of bliss to be attained by mere evolutionary progress in the course of ages. We might ascend from one heavenly state to the next, and then to the next and to the next, ascending from heaven to neaven, as we climb rung upon rung of a ladder, without ever reaching Nibbana. If we were to leave millions of heavens below us—as we have already done—we would still be as far from Nibbana as when we started, for in that direction Nibbana does not lie. Nibbana, then, is neither a heavenly condition, nor but another step upon the ladder of evolution.

There is another misconception current with regard to Nibbana, namely that it is a dreamless sleep that lasts throughout eternity. Such a conception constitutes but another example of the ignorance on the part of those who insist upon accounting for Nibbana in terms of their own daily experience; on the part of those who cannot bring themselves to realize that it is a state which it would be almost useless to attempt to describe to them: for those who feel it will, of course, understand at once, whilst those who do not, can hardly be made to understand.

We are not yet at the end of the series of current misapprehensions regarding the nature of Nibbana. There are those that maintain that it cannot be experienced until after the death of the body, in face of the fact that the Buddha and all his Arhats attained long before the crumbling of the physical frame. Then there are such as believe that the indication of the existence of Nibbana is but a bait held out to the deluded disciple in order to recruit him to the body of adherents to the doctrine and the precepts, a promise of ultimate happiness, a reward of nebulous bliss for having faithfully lived a life of solitary moral asceticism whilst propagating the system. Still others, utterly permeated with the theory of evolution as applied to world systems and world cycles, entertain the idea that it is possible for human beings so rapidly to fulfil the requirements of their evolutionary programme as to outstrip their fellow humans by immense periods of time, and that, having reached the end of the particular cycle of evolution, they will then await in a condition of extreme bliss the advent of their brethren at the goal set before them, whereupon they all together will start upon a new cycle of evolution, this period of blissful waiting being regarded as the state of Nibbana; upon the same principle that a group of people climbing a mountain are outstripped by a few who reach the top ahead of the others, there to enjoy a well-deserved rest until the remainder of the party shall have caught up with them when, after having partaken of refreshment, they all prepare to descend into the next valley whence the next mountain is to be attempted. The thought of such endless migration from life to life, from world to world ; the endlessness of such a struggle "might well fill the heart even of the bravest with a shudder at the resultlessness of all this unending course of things".

Needless to say, all such theories, though in some respects applicable to evolutionary progression, are altogether inapplicable to the attainment of Nibbana, and their acceptance constitutes no inconsiderable obstacle to the treading of the Path, the Noble Eightfold Path, leading Thereto.

The Beyondless Security : The liberation spoken of in reference to Nibbana is not but the temporary liberation referred to by some of the theories above enumerated. However long such heavenly joys may last, they must ultimately come to an end. Relatively speaking they are of no more importance than the evanescent pleasures of physical existence and as much to be eschewed. Such temporary relief from woe is the working of kamma and not the end of kamma. It is the consequence of accumulated energy which has liberated itself in that particular direction, whereas the Buddhist aims at a condition which is neither the working of kamma nor its development, but one in which kamma has no place whatsoever, to which kamma is altogether foreign.

This is clearly to be seen from the expressions by which Nibbana is often designated. It is called "The Ever Tranquil State," "The Unshaken Condition," "The Deathless," "The Non-Deceasing," "The Beyond End," "The Final Security," "The Apprehensionless"; all names expressive of a condition that leaves no room either for progression or for retrogression, for return to a previous condition or for entrance upon a new state of existence of any kind.

Nibbana may be described as a state of balance, of composure, of the neutralization of opposing forces. The forces of nature that are constantly creating friction, that are producing the world by virtue of that friction, are here neutralized. He who has attained Nibbana knows of no time, no self, no woe. Must we say that there is no time left? We may say that there is no further sense of time. Is there no self left? There is no further sense of self. Is there no woe left? There is no further sense of woe. The world of our own making has disappeared, vanished, together with the disappearance, the vanishing of our sense of time, of self, of suffering. Our sense of time is the succession of events as we see them, as we respond to them: it is a panoramic sequence of our consecutive states of consciousness; it is

* 10

the consciousness of that sequence. A man who falls into a swoon thinks that the moment he awakes is the moment succeeding the one in which he fainted away. His sense of succession has not been interrupted. As we manage to ignore our selves, as during moments of intense activity, excitement, or thought, our sense of the passing of time also diminishes, and our sense of joy correspondingly increases. If we were able to forget our selves entirely, why, there would be no further sense of time, which would be equivalent to the most intense bliss. And the permanent condition of selflessness, of timelessness, of joy inexpressible, constitutes Nibbana.

Nibbana, therefore, is the capacity to understand that the world as we see it is of our own creating. As we respond to impacts from without physically, emotionally, or mentally, we construct for ourselves the universe. We do this by means of the mechanism provided by the khandhas. Thus we become conscious simultaneously of the self and of the world, of the within and the without, just as we can know darkness only by our recognition of light. Where there is no further sense of self, no sense of time, there is no world, no panorama of succession, no pageant of events. With the dissociation of the khandhas the world dissolves, friction disappears, and only bliss remains. We have undone our knot on the string of life and, having ceased to assert ourselves, we have given relief to the tension in the lives of the other members of humanity, the adjoining knots on the string. We have truly sacrificed ourselves for the sake of mankind, for we have dissolved the I by relaxing our hold upon self, by permitting it to be pulled back from a complex knot into the simple string. Is this annihilation? It is, indeed, the annihilation of the feeling of self, of the necessity to become other, of the drive to go further, to climb higher, to aim at the unachieved. It is also the annihilation of suffering, of pain, of distress, of sorrow, of woe, of friction, of strain. Or perhaps we should say it is the removal of these things. Just as a cataract is removed from the eye and sight is restored, so this annihilation, this removal, leaves a sense of joy inexpressible, of peace indescribable, of security unimaginable. And it is this sense of utter joy, of utter peace, of utter security, that constitutes Nibbana!

How can we attain to this sense of joy, of peace, and of security? Our answer is not "By faith in God," although we recognize that by such faith, such feelings in a measure are emphasized. But in a measure only. Just as a man who is in need of diversion and rest may go to another climate or to the seaside and may benefit by the change, but if he stays there long enough he will soon again need diversion and rest; so faith in God, beautiful though it is, is no permanent remedy for the evil of existence, for the roots of this evil lie deeper. The child may find security in its mother's arms and be perfectly happy there. Even so the child mind may take refuge in the bosom of the Deity, and find comfort therein. But does the child know aught of its mother's sorrows and difficulties? Hardly, for she moves in a world that the child cannot understand. Does the child mind know aught of the sorrows and difficulties the Deity has to contend with in managing his universe? Hardly, for He moves in a world that the undeveloped mind cannot comprehend.

The Buddha proclaims the futility of seeking peace where no ultimate peace is to be found. For the Deity Himself is not at peace. How can he be with a suffering world on his hands? As we are individually responsible for what befalls us, so we must seek peace by doing away with those conditions that are constituents of sorrow, of distress, of misunderstanding.

The Four Intoxications: We are clearly told what those conditions are. They are called intoxications, for like drug or drink they befuddle the mind, exalt the self, and lift things out of their proper perspective, just as coloured and faultily adjusted eyeglasses distort the vision. The first of these intoxications is sensuality, a condition in which the pleasures of the senses are given primary importance until such delights as are not directly sense pleasures, the more spiritual joys, have no further attraction. The second of the intoxications is the desire for existence, physical or superphysical. Such desire obviously does not aid us to recognize the value of self-sacrifice, particularly that of such utter sacrifice of self as is advocated by the Buddhist system. The third of the intoxications is ignorance, the ignorance that refuses knowledge, that causes us to stumble and slip, that is lazy and inert. The fourth and last of the intoxications is that of prejudiced views, of theorizing upon insufficient data. This is the kind of ignorance that refuses further knowledge, clings to false notions : more damaging than the ignorance that asks for no knowledge at all, just as the drinking of gin to quench one's thirst is far more injurious than not drinking at all.

He who understands the nature of these four intoxications : sensuality, desire of existence, ignorance, and fanaticism, will of his own accord thoroughly appreciate to what extent they impede his progress along the Path to Nibbana, and will seriously endeavour to eliminate those obstacles therefrom. Sensuality and desire for existence both fall under the head of craving ; ignorance and fanaticism under the head of ignorance. And what has been said concerning either craving or ignorance can be read in preceding chapters. At any rate, the four intoxications must be totally renounced and overcome before the notion concerning the nature of Nibbana can penetrate our understanding.

The Necessary Efforts: Together with the endeavour to eliminate the four intoxications, positive efforts must be made to bring about a state of balance, of composure. Definite exercises are prescribed to this end. After the poisonous influences or sensuality, desire for existence, ignoance and fanatical notions to some extent have been removed, and the mental perspective of things has become somewhat less distorted, the mind may be trained in concentration until such mental concentration becomes habitual and the attention once directed does not any longer easily wander. The mentality must be mastered and ruled and may not any longer run away with our attention. This is the first step. The next step is the tranquillization of the mind through such concentration. In the third effort complete equanimity is attained such as cannot be disturbed except by the will of the person experiencing it. The fourth step is the attainment of pure mindfulness, wherein the mind is "concentrated, purified, pliant and fit," a condition which it is difficult adequately to describe. Each of these exercises is in the nature of a trance and they are consecutive, that is to say it is not possible to reach, say the fourth stage without having passed through the first, second and third. There is no loss of consciousness in these states: on the contrary, the consciousness of attainment is vivid and strong, as is that of the bliss attendant upon each of them. They are "filled with zest and pleasurable emotion," as the scriptures have it. Through these exercises the mind that before was the victim of the current of events now becomes its master.

From concentrated and reasoned thinking springs joy, thence zest, thence composure, thence happiness, thence true concentratedness; and by such concentratedness we see and know things as they really are. Thus seeing and knowing, there arises within us first distaste, then passionlessness, then freedom. In this way these exercises lead to liberation.

Similarly these trance states break up any remnant we may have of a belief in a permanent and fundamental higher self or ego, through eliminating all mental self-emphasis. Any exercises in concentration or trance states based upon or connected with the slightest emphasis upon the feeling of self are severely condemned in the Buddhist regime, as they necessarily must lead to further entanglement and away from the set goal to the extent that the self-feeling is emphasized and that the consequent elation is one of self-satisfaction. All such practices as lead us to say: "I am I"; "I am God"; "I am the Universe"; "I am the Great Self"; etc., as advocated in the New Thought and allied movements, are as so much dross thrown in with the Buddhist grain. Such affirmations represent a mind involved in "I-making," in "mine-making conceit," and as such a mind that is incapable of realizing the fundamental principle of Buddhist psychology, namely that of the necessity of self-sacrifice for the sake of suffering mankind, quite independently of the ultimate advantage that of necessity must accrue to the man who follows the precepts of the Noble Eightfold Path.

There is another set of exercises equally important. Just as those described are exercises for the mind, so is there a similar set of four exercises for the heart. In the first of these we sit down and meditate upon love, fill ourselves with love, pour out love in all directions, to all creatures, towards all that lives. In the second exercise we meditate upon sympathy, fill ourselves with sympathy, pour out sympathy in all directions, to all creatures, towards all that lives. In the third exercise we meditate upon pity, fill ourselves with pity, pour out pity in all directions, to all creatures, towards all that lives. In the fourth exercise we attain to a state of equanimity of heart. Having through our love for all beings felt their sufferings with them and pitied them therefor, our equanimity is not based upon indifference but upon the recognition that only by such equanimity, such imperturbability, can we really help the world at large. Our love as such does not help: it but induces our sympathy, our fellow-suffering. Our sympathy as such does not help: it but serves to arouse our pity. Even our pity, though it may stir us to action, is of little value unless it is superseded by presence of mind or equanimity. If my brother whom I love breaks his arm, my sympathy for his pain will cause me to pity him, but neither my love, nor my sympathy, nor my pity will be of any value to him unless I have sufficient presence of mind, sufficient equanimity to know what steps to take to alleviate his suffering. My crying, my wailing, my rushing about and tearing my hair, is so much wasted energy, so much lost motion. I must control my feelings, remain perfectly calm, make a tourniquet, adjust it properly and take him to where further medical aid can be obtained. So it is with the four heart exercises in point. Through my love for all that lives I learn to realize the world's pain and sorrow, and my deepest and most heartfelt pity is the natural consequence. Now how can I aid this poor suffering world ? How can I contribute my share towards alleviating the pain I see and feel everywhere about me ? I cannot take upon my shoulders the kamma of others. As each must digest his own food, so each is forced to undo his own kamma, for he has himself produced it. But I can tell him how to prevent future sorrow and transmit to him the Buddha's Message. In addition I begin to understand that the very fact of my self-existence adds to the collective sorrow, and that therefore I must sacrifice myself for the sake of the world at large. That is the most effective help I can render. To go about "healing" is a mere temporary expedient: it is like raising a pig for the slaughter, for the person "healed" has not learned the law that governed the origin of his ill and may fall into the same pit again. The story is told of the widow who, coming to the Buddha with her dead child in her arms, asked Him to resuscitate it and was directed by the Wise One to obtain a handful of mustard seed from a house in the village where no death had occurred and return to him with it. The poor woman went from house to house, and although mustard seed there was a plenty, not a single dwelling could be found where no death had taken place. Finally realizing that death was a visitor in every family, she disembarrassed herself of the already decomposing body of the babe which in her mad grief she had held tightly clasped to her breast in the course of her search, and returned enlightened and at peace to where the Buddha was, became one of his most ardent adherents, and attained the state of Arahat in the same life.

Self-Sacrifice: In view of such considerations I decide that I must renounce, yea, sacrifice my own self for the sake of the suffering world, and as I reach this understanding by means of and with the equanimity of heart that I have been cultivating, I also set about to attain Nibbana as soon as I may. The state of equanimity now becomes one of composure, of balance, of neutralization of the forces that have produced the friction which I know as my I. "Just as, Bhikkhus, from the juxtaposition and friction of two sticks warmth is generated, heat is born; and from the altering, the relinquishing of just those sticks that corresponding warmth is allayed and ceases, even so does sensation arise because of contact capable of producing it, and cease when the contact ceases." So the friction which I know as my self, my I, will cease when the contact producing it ceases. And by relinquishing this contact I induce a state of equanimity, of balance, of composure. In this way I contribute to the balance of the world at large, just as a person at the centre of a see-saw, though himself not in motion, yet helps to stabilize its swing and to lighten the shock with which the ends strike the ground by having transferred his weight from the end of the see-saw to the middle of it. To reach the centre, the balancing point of the see-saw of life, that constitutes Nibbana.

Yet in spite of the fact that I now have sacrificed my self, I have not lost anything worth losing. On the contrary, I have gained what never before I had been able to gain, namely unalloyed and undiminishable delight. Here is the bliss of attainment without satiety. Nibbana has been pronounced fair and lovely to a degree unattainable by a mere spell of celestial existence. The gods themselves have not tasted its joy. Nibbana means final attainment. Nothing remains to be pursued and it is thoroughly realized that the delusion that joy lies mainly in pursuing is but a pathetic way of trying to reconcile ourselves to failure. In Nibbana we find true emancipation, true liberty, true knowledge, true insight. The scales have fallen from our eyes and now for the first time we truly see. We have renounced the self and have gained The Peace.

Thus it is clearly to be seen that the not infrequent accusation that the person who seeks to gain Nibbana is working for purely selfish ends, that he is cowardly leaving the world to its sorrow and extracting himself from the woe of existence, is utterly groundless. For how can one be selfish by sacrificing self ? And if this sacrifice of self is made for the sake of the world, by virtue of the recognition that such sacrifice is the only way *effectively* to aid the world and humanity at large, that the relief of suffering can never be accomplished through shouldering the responsibility of others, or by having others shoulder our own responsibility, then surely the last shred of such an accusation must disappear. For such sacrifice of self requires the utmost courage, determination and exertion !

Nor can Buddhism be declared a religion of pessimism, simply because it condemns life as we know it. For recognizing evil and sorrow, we do not in principle teach resignation to it, but rather revolt to and escape from its domination once and for all. This escape is called Nibbana, and the Path to this escape is the Noble Middle Path.

The Attainment: On the Path there are four tages, each stage culminating in a definite sense of attainment, in the knowledge of attainment, in the consciousness of attainment. We know when we have entered upon the current towards escape, though it is possible that several more lives are still required until we reach the goal. This knowledge is called the fruit of the first stage, and the person who has this certainty the " Current-Attainer ". We also know when we have progressed along the Path sufficiently to be certain that only one more incarnatian is required to attain to the final consummation. This knowledge is called the fruit of the second stage, and the person who has this certainty is called the " Once-Returning ". Again we are aware when the Path has been followed so far that it is quite possible to attain Nibbana in this very existence without the necessity of carrying over anything to a subsequent life. The person having this certainty is referred to as the " Never-Returning," and the certainty of this condition is the fruit of the third stage. The fruit of the fourth stage is the state of Arahat, that is to say it is the actual attainment of Nibbana. The stream of existence has been crossed and the other shore has been reached !

It has been a source of considerable difficulty to many who have discussed the question of Nibbana how its attainment can be possible without the immediate death and dissolution of the bodily manifestation. This, however, may be explained in the following manner. The khandhas, the constituents of the individuality, hold together by the very strain they exercise upon each other, just as a house of cards remains standing by virtue of the pressure the cards are mutually sustaining. Extract one of the supporting cards, and the entire structure will fall to pieces. Some moments will elapse, however, between the removal of the card and the collapse of the structure. So when the hold of the khandhas upon each other is loosened, some time will elapse before the individuality finally dissolves. Or suppose I keep a wheel spinning by turning a handle. As soon as I let go of the handle the force which made it spin is no longer being applied. But it will be some time before it comes to a standstill. Even so the body need not necessarily collapse the very moment Nibbana is attained, for though the force of craving is no longer turning the handle of the wheel of self-existence, the wheel must run its course before it can finally come to rest.

It is true, therefore, that a last change is still due. This must occur upon the death of the body, when what is called Parinibbana sets in, that is to say Utter Nibbana, when nothing observable remains. How this can be reconciled with the idea that there is no annihilation can perhaps be explained by the simile of the glowing spark which, when whirled around, appears as a circle, but when the whirling lessens and gradually ceases, the true nature of the spark is recognized and the illusion that there existed a continuous circle disappears. The circle has been annihilated, but there really never was a circle: there was only a circular motion. Thus it is that in reality we are aware only of what is not, and that only upon the attainment of Nibbana the exact truth concerning the nature of existence becomes perfectly clear to us.

It is a very curious fact that recently scientific philosophy has turned in the direction of the old Buddhist concepts. Einstein's law of relativity to a great extent corroborates our notions concerning Nibbana, at any rate in so far as it is based upon the recognition that time and space are not the absolute entities upon which the moving systems of the universe were dependent, as they were proclaimed to be by Galileo and Newton, but that time and space in every instance are relative to such moving systems. To use Einstein's own words: " Till now it was believed that time and space existed by themselves, even if there was nothing else—no sun, no earth, no stars; while now we know that time and space are not the vessel for the universe, but could not exist at all if there were no contents—namely, no sun, earth, and other celestial bodies." How curiously this view coincides with the Buddhist notion of time and space can only be appreciated by the student. And Nibbana is the condition wherein time and space, and incidentally the world, have utterly disappeared.

Does this mean that there is nothing left? Says the Buddha, replying to a similar question put to him by one of his followers: "Illustrious disciple, Nibbana is not like the pitcher not yet made out of the clay, nor is it like the pitcher which has been broken; nor is it like the horn of the hare, or the hair of the tortoise, that is to say something purely imaginary. But it may be compared to the absence of something different from itself. Illustrious disciple, as you say, although the ox has no quality of the horse in it, yet you cannot say that the ox does not exist. Nibbana is just so. In the midst of sorrow there is no Nibbana, and in Nibbana there is no sorrow. So we may justly define Nibbana as that sort of state which prevails by the absence of something essentially different from itself." Thus we see that, though all that has disappeared that can be described in terms familiar to us, the state of

Nibbana is an actual condition which, by virtue of the fact that no sorrow, distress, friction, or woe of any sort can penetrate there, we can only refer to as a state of utter and ineffable bliss.

In another simile the Buddha expresses himself concerning the effect of death upon a person after the attainment of Nibbana. "The case may be compared to a river's bank along which different trees and shrubs are growing. Suddenly the river rises, and by its rapid flow carries everything before it into the great ocean—all except the supple willow which, by its yielding character, is saved."

The Choice: Now in the history of each human race there is a period which roughly may be called the turning point, where the race as a whole has reached the zenith of its physical organization and where social consciousness begins to take the place of individual development; the period at which a new unit is beginning to form itself out of the collective units constituting the human race. It is exactly at this point that the Buddha makes His appearance to induce such a portion of mankind as He may, to tread the Path to Salvation and to turn away from the otherwise necessary social organization in which every human being is to become an integral unit in the organism to be composed of collective humanity.

There are two kinds of social organization. The one kind is that based on law and compulsion,

* 11

and we find it to a very great extent prevailing in the older civilizations, in which the king is the head of a ruling hierarchy which the people are virtually forced to maintain, whether it is their will or not. It is the autocratic or patriarchal kind of government.

The other kind is a social organization depending upon voluntary co-operation on the part of the people. It is based upon the recognition by each individual in the state that he must do his part towards keeping the social ball rolling. This is the kind of social state that is to prevail in the future. It is the democratic or fratriarchal kind of government.

It is obvious that the former cannot be transformed into the latter all at once. Figuring the course of a humanity at some millions of years, the period of transition from the one condition to the other, from world autocracy to world democracy, may take a few, perhaps three or four thousand years. And it is during this period of transition that the appeal of Buddhism is strongest, for it is the time at which man has the choice between continuing his human progression towards godhood, and taking the necessary steps to attain Nibbana. In each successive humanity it always is at the beginning of this period of transition that a Buddha appears to proclaim to mankind the existence of Nibbana, of Liberation, and the Way Thereto, the Noble Eightfold Path. Those of humanity that wish to take advantage of the opportunity now can do so and make the necessary efforts required to escape out of the evolutionary net. Those that do not, will continue along the road of evolutionary progression until they shall have reached the corresponding period in the next higher kingdom, that of the Devas or Angels, where once again they shall have a similar opportunity within the reign of the next Buddha, and so on.

There is just one more point in connection with the concept of Nibbana that will have to be explained. Thus far we have been dealing only with individual salvation, that is to say with the attainment of Nibbana by members of the human race and of the higher kingdoms in comparatively small numbers. There is, however, one other method of attaining Nibbana, and that is by waiting until the God of this entire world system, in whose body we are but cells, shall himself reach Nibbana. In the meantime we may advance and progress and participate in the world which He is trying to bring to perfection. This process, of course, from our point of view of time, will be sensed as taking many, many ages of immense duration, although to Him it may represent but a few lives. That our Logos finally will attain Nibbana, of course there is no doubt. It is this concept which has caused so much misunderstanding concerning the meaning of Nibbana in certain sections of the Orient, and has developed into the body of Mahayanists, or those who intend to attain Nibbana by means of the Great Vehicle, that is to say the great vehicle represented by the God of this world system of which we form part, as distinct from the Hinayanists or those who intend to attain Nibbana without waiting until the God of this world system shall be ready to make the Great Effort, but who intend to make the effort independently of Him by means of the Little Vehicle, that is to say their own individual raft. Christianity, perhaps somewhat more so in its original form than in its medieval and modern garb, is but a branch of the Mahayanist movement, as can clearly be discerned by all who will take the trouble to acquaint themselves with the more accurate translations of the Greek Testament that have appeared in the course of the last decade or two and with the innumerable concurrences in Mahayana Buddhism and in Christianity.

In these studies, however, we are dealing exclusively with the original Hinayana Buddhism, the Theravada or Teaching of the Elders, which expounds the path towards individual salvation. For the Buddha brought the message that it is not necessary to wait and suffer during all those thousands of ages, as our time sense goes, that it would have to take the Deity of this world system to attain Liberation. He in His turn might be awaiting the Nibbana of the next higher Deity, in Whose body He is a cell in His turn, just as we are cells in the body of the former. If the Deity of this world system Himself follows the Hinayana system, the method of the Small Vehicle, that is if He strives to attain Nibbana without waiting for the attainment of His World-God, then surely we may follow His example and also pursue the method of the Small Vehicle, that is the Path of the Elders, ourselves. If, on the other hand, He is not, if He is following the Mahayana system, the method of waiting for Nibbana until His Godhead shall strive to attain, then surely it will be by far our wiser course *not* to wait until this is accomplished, for it would take an immensity of world cycles before such consummation might take place. For the fact remains that we do not *have* to wait. Indeed, it will distinctly aid our Deity to have us contribute to the balance of His world by our reaching the condition of Nibbana; to such an extent, it is said, that all the Angels and Devas rejoice each time one of us attains, and that mankind also vastly benefits thereby.

Nibbana, then, is not so much a desire to be cultivated as a goal to be attained. It is the sacrifice of the state of unbalancement which we call Self, to be followed—not because one desires it, but simply because it happens to be the case—

by unspeakable bliss, by "the peace that passeth all understanding". The road thereto is the Noble Middle Path; the condition therefor is consistent and untiring effort; and the most necessary requirement therein is utter self-renunciation.

THE UNIVERSE

TO us human beings the universe is a unification of dissociated impressions, a unification which originates our world, which solidifies for us our environment, which makes of us a specific reagent entity. If we will but realize that the dissociations are many and the associations comparatively few, we shall see how flimsy is this world which we regard so solemnly and as of so much importance! If we could but realize that with different associations we would live in a different world, that the entire universe is but our own reactive capacity, and that our entire self is but a centre of responsiveness, we should see things as they are rather than as they but appear.

Suppose we were conscious of the ultra-violet light emanations in addition to what we regard as our present normal vision. It is obvious that under such conditions most things which now are transparent, such as glass and crystal, would become opaque; and many substances now opaque, such as wood and paper, would become transparent. What an entirely different world it would be! We could hardly draw a comparison between that world and the one we now inhabit. The very appearance of the objects would have changed and would call for an entirely different adjustment of our reactive faculties.

Suppose we could thus change our vision from the normal to that comprising a reaction to the ultra-violet rays, and exercised this faculty upon a specific set of objects, say a living room with its appropriate furniture and decorations, we would hardly be able to recognize the same set of objects and their purposes.

Let us drive this example a step further. If, instead of merely seeing the ultra-violet emanations we became aware of an entirely new set of radiations, which, one in respect to the other, held the same relation as do the ultra-violet to the rays to which we are accustomed. Had we such vision, then indeed the world would be a different place and we would speak of it most likely not as the same world differently seen, but as an entirely different world perhaps co-existing with or interpenetrating our present sphere of consciousness. The truth, of course, would be very simple: it is the same world of which we would be seeing a little more than we are seeing now. And may there not exist beings who possess such wider vision and whose consciousness, even though it were accessible, would be entirely unintelligible to us?

We see now why Buddhism lays so much stress on the fact that with our thought and feeling and action we are thinking and feeling and acting as from the purely human standpoint; that this human standpoint itself varies somewhat according to each individual human being or set of khandhas; and that only the most fundamental generalities hold good for man as a particular class of entity.

Man's awareness or consciousness comprises a limited set of colours and forms, of sensations, of perceptions, and of tendencies, and it is for every man to decide whether he will be limited by these or whether he will refuse to accept his accustomed limitations and expand his consciousness in unaccustomed directions. If he chooses the latter he can do so in two ways: he can force a widening of his regular avenues of perception and develop the higher sight (clairvoyance), the higher hearing (clairaudience), and other out of the ordinary faculties referred to in Buddhist writings as the Lower Iddhi; or else he may refuse to deal with his sense organs as the means towards the expansion of his consciousness and simply emphasize the development of the faculties of his understanding, thus paving the way to what is known as the Higher Iddhi. The faculties indicated by this more lofty appellation so utterly transcend human and even divine consciousness that the very gods themselves may be said to covet them. For they have reached their god stations along the path of faculty expansion, and however much their sense faculties have expanded in relation to *their* particular spheres of existence, they cannot be regarded as any further favoured than we are in relation to *our* particular world. The follower of the Buddha, therefore, realizing this, very wisely refuses to go the way of the gods, though he respects those whose call it is to do so, as also those whose call it has been in the past and who now hold very lofty offices in the hierarchy of evolving beings. The Buddhist rather turns to the path of the Higher Iddhi, the Path leading to Nibbana. He sets about understanding the nature of his experiences. He rummages through the content of his consciousness and eliminates the superfluous material. Above all, he realizes that it is the stress of self which produces all other stress, physical as well as mental, emotional as well as spiritual. He understands the nature of the self and he also understands that all self-tension increases the interweaving of the khandhas who will let go of each other or of the kamma which they enclasp as little as the fingers of a dead man's hand will release a pebble they tightly clutch. It is only by relaxation, by a loss of the sense of self, that the ultimate object can be achieved. No clasping, no grasping whether physical, emotional, mental, or spiritual—will bring or even contribute to salvation from the wheel of the torture of alternate living and dying, getting and losing, plenty and want !

Being and Becoming: The fundamental attitude of the Buddhist towards the universe is that of the realization that all that he sees, that he understands, is in a condition of change and transience. The very gods and their heavens are transient; existing, it is true, for longer periods in their present condition than do we ourselves, but not, on that account, eternally. When we speak of the eternal, the infinite, we speak like a little child that can count to ten and no further, and then says "infinite". So, simply because the periods of existence of other sets of beings are beyond human comprehension, that is no reason to assign to them eternal and changeless being. The Buddhist in all apparent Being sees but continuous Becoming, unending change; never permanence. And, he reasons, where there is no permanence there can be no permanent happiness either. Where there are changes in happiness, there must be room for unhappiness, for misery, for suffering, for pain; there can be no fearless and comfortable existence except in moments of thoughtlessness and mental blindness and torpitude. And mental blindness and torpitude must be avoided by all means, for that kind of folly, though producing selfish satisfaction, must also come to an end sooner or later when the mental eye refuses to remain closed and once again opens to a world immersed in utter misery. We can be happy only by closing our eyes to the pain of others, but we cannot keep them closed. The sooner we open them, therefore, and arouse from our selfish lethargy, the less we will have to regret, to have remorse over, to retrace. And that is the call of the Buddha : " Open your eyes, that ye may see!" Wherever we may look, no Being can be discovered : we find one huge fermenting mass of Becoming! To suppose a fundamental, changeless, absolute Being behind all this Becoming is to do violence to our intelligence, for how can something changeless, stable, absolute, eternal, have any logical connection with something changeful, moving, relative, and transient? The very connection would impair the changelessness of the Changeless!

Now the Buddha most clearly saw how the matter stood. Instead of accepting the prevailing Brahmin view of an Ultimate Being behind the phenomena of Becoming, He apprehended unceasing Becoming without a substratum of Being. But He also perceived that there was a way for us, without pursuing the phantom of Being, to get out of the world of change into a condition of changelessness that had nothing whatsoever to do with the notion of Eternal Being. It is this that constitutes the Great Secret of the Buddha. By giving up our Self we can give up the World. Having given up my Self, " this world is no more ". Not then by expanding the Self until it embraces the whole universe—as impossible an achievement as it is to count one, two, three, and so on, to the end of the numerical system—but by the utter effacement of the Self, the sacrifice of the Self, the loss of the Self, can the changeless state be found: not by identification with a supposed Changeless Being, nor by complete annihilation, but by establishing a mean of the nature of neither Being nor Non-Being can a balance be struck. It is this which brings the world to an end, which eradicates pain, which utterly destroys suffering!

The Buddhist view of the Universe is twofold: objective, or as seen from without; and subjective, or as seen from within. We shall first deal with the objective view, and then with the subjective.

The Objective View: Viewing the world through the windows of our senses we see ourselves surrounded by a variety of beings and objects which we classify according to the likeness they bear to us.

We first realize the existence of immense numbers of other human entities constituted more or less like ourselves. We must never lose sight of the fact that the total of our fellow-members of the human race aggregates to from fifteen to sixteen hundred millions, a figure not easily accurately conceived by the mind.

Next to the human kingdom of the earth we have the animal kingdom. An extraordinary number of animals populates this globe who, in their constitution, vary from nearly human entities to almost shapeless single cells.

We next have the plant kingdom, even more varied than the animal world, ranging from trees and complex flowering plants to cell-like structures that hardly fall within the range of our observation.

The division next in order is the mineral world which, if not greater in variety than the plant kingdom, is even more widely distributed, as the very earth itself is composed of mineral matter.

The human, animal, plant and mineral regions are the kingdoms that, as a rule, fall within the direct scope of our vision. This, of course, does not mean that our earth has not other modes of life as well. There are regions below the mineral, as there are kingdoms beyond the human. Generally speaking, however, these kingdoms are not within the range of our observation, for the senses with which we perceive are rarely capable of responding to impacts emanating from any other than the four regions enumerated.

There are exceptions, however. There are men and women whose senses are so sensitive, either naturally or made so by training, that they can perceive substance of regions below the mineral world, as well as beings of a higher order than those of the human kingdom. And it is through their testimony, given in many instances independently from each other, that we may learn of these higher and lower worlds of life. It is quite within the scope of the possible that we ourselves can train our own senses to such perceptions. Many people are actually doing so at the present day, as it has been done throughout the ages, and there are even schools where the development and the refinement of the human senses are being taught.

Through similar testimony we know that, in addition to the world of which we have cognizance during our hours of waking consciousness, there are other worlds on our earth which are closely related to this one. If we may refer to this plane of existence as the physical or material plane—though the other worlds are as physical and material as this—we may say that the plane most closely interwoven with it is the emotional world, composed of material of a different order, to which we respond through certain nerve centres and through which our emotions and feelings work: whence its name. In that world we also have a range of kingdoms similar to that in this physical world, of which we may become independently aware by detaching our emotional organization from our physical, as we may do in sleep, dream and trance states, unconsciously as a rule, but consciously by practice.

Again there is the mental world—as material and as physical as this or the emotional world—with which we are connected through the brain and other nerve centres and through which our thoughts work. Its substance is of a different order from that of the world of which we are ordinarily conscious through our senses: but in this world also the range of kingdoms does not materially differ. If we learn to detach our mental make-up from our bodily, we may become independently aware of this mental sphere also.

We recognize, then, on this earth three different worlds: a material sense world, an emotional world, and a mental one. It is in these three worlds that we live and feel and think; that our senses work, and that we respond to the impress upon our senses. Through our perceptions we recognize the form world; through our sensations we are connected with the emotional world; whilst our response tendencies have their origin in the mental world. The consciousness binds together the form world, our perceptions, sensations, and response tendencies into a congruous and connected whole.

Just as we may speak of the physical world as a limited region—limited in the sense that there are regions outside it and different from it—so the emotional and mental worlds are regions that have their own limits, and we participate only in very small degree in their manifestation. They interpenetrate and each has its own sub-regions, its own kingdoms, and its own inhabitants. These latter may sometimes communicate with the inhabitants of this world, as people of our world may on occasion get into touch with them. But generally speaking each region has its own octave of responsiveness.

Now this same set of regions is repeated on each of the planets of this solar system ; in fact, on each of the planets of other solar systems as well. That does not mean that life on other planets is the exact counterpart of life on earth. That would hardly be likely seeing that there are such considerable differences in conditions of atmosphere, temperature, gravitation, etc. But in a general way the same principles hold good. There is the physical, the emotional, and the mental life, each in its own stage of organization and complexity, interacting and together forming the three worlds in which the five khandhas combine into the corresponding units of self-consciousness in the sub-mineral, mineral, plant, animal, human, and superhuman kingdoms.

Each solar system again has its own family of planets. Thus there are many solar systems that together form what might be called a Cosmic System. Again there are numerous cosmic systems that together form a still greater system, having each its central sun and its planetary worlds with their corresponding inhabitants. This series extends upward indefinitely.

But just as there is a series of increasing magnitude, so is there a series of decreasing size. Just as each solar system has its planets, so each molecule of physical, emotional, or mental matter is a solar system of which the atoms constitute the planets. Small though these be from our human point of view, in their own fields they are, relatively speaking, as large as is the earth, and they have their inhabitants, just as have the larger planets, as well as the three worlds through which such beings function. Each of these molecular solar systems with its atomic planets is composed of an immeasurable number of still smaller systems of worlds, and so this downward series continues without conceivable end. That which is immensely large from one standpoint, is infinitesimal from another. Relatively speaking, however, there is no essential difference between say, the earth and its inhabitants and the atom and its inhabitants. As a matter of fact our earth is but an atom of the molecule that we refer to as our solar system, which in its turn helps to constitute the material of a larger world.

Let us quote from some of the Buddhist writings : " One sun illumines with its brightness one world. A thousand worlds have their thousand suns, each having its own set of regions. All these collectively are referred to as a small chiliocosm (' thousand-world '). A thousand small chiliocosms constitute a medium chiliocosm, and a thousand medium chiliocosms constitute a Great Chiliocosm ; so that in a Great Chiliocosm there are a thousand million suns, etc. Such a collection of worlds constitutes *a single universe.* But beyond this, in the immensity of space, there are such Great Chiliocosms in each of the ten regions (N., NE., E., SE., S., SW., W., NW., Zenith and Nadir)." In another scripture, referring to the same subject, we read: "In the western region, passing over ten myriads of lakhs of universes, there is a world called 'The Inconceivably Happy'." Again we read: "With regard to the situation of this happy system in reference to our own universe, it is due west more than ten myriads of lakhs of universes. And, if we regard the position of this happy region in reference to the surrounding universes, it is situated in the thirteenth tier, regarding our own universe as in the middle of this tier; then westward, a distance corresponding to worlds as numerous as the grains of dust in an entire system, is situated this border universe of the thirteenth tiêr called 'The Inconceivably Happy'." In still another book we find the following: "In the midst of an illimitable ocean are the innumerable oceans of worlds scattered throughout space." "The number of worlds which lie scattered throughout one single tier is beyond the power of words to express. Above our tier, after passing an innumerable set of systems of worlds, there is a second tier, and so on for twenty tiers. In the very midst of the thirteenth tier is the system we inhabit. To the extreme west of our tier, after passing universe systems incalculable for number, is a universe called 'The Inconceivably Happy'. Thus towards each of the ten regions of space there are similar tiers of universe systems. These again are surrounded by others, incalculable for number, all being contained within the illimitable ocean above named. And in the same manner similar oceans stretch towards each of the ten points of space."

How far removed is such a conception from the narrow view of creation still widely prevalent and maintained amongst the less informed in our western countries!

From this it can be seen what an infinitesimal speck of dust a solar system represents in the Buddhist imagination. Yet each solar system not only has its three regions with its corresponding kingdoms of entities who rise in the scale towards godhood, but is governed, maintained and pervaded by its Ruler, the God of the System. Thus also each minor, medium, and great chiliocosm has its God, and even these combine to form still mightier universes utterly beyond human comprehension.

From this point of view, what would it avail a human being to enter upon the path towards godhood? Why continue to struggle in this mess of cosmic pottage? Even if there be an entire universe with conditions infinitely superior to those prevailing here, and on that account denominated "The Inconceivably Happy," and even granted the utterly remote possibility that some of us might succeed in transferring ourselves there, the difficulties besetting the Path to Nibbana would be considerably smaller than the realization of such a transfer, and the happiness of Nibbana considerably greater, just as the happiness of the free and detached bhikkhu is greatly superior to that of the well-nigh all-powerful monarch.

It may well be asked, however, how we know that the descriptions of world systems and universes quoted above are correct. Our reply is that this is of very little importance. What is of importance in this regard is not whether the notions of the Buddhist writers concerning the extension and classification of the universe are accurate, but rather *that such notions prevail* ! For their prevalence is a sure antidote to narrow-mindedness and to what we might call cosmic provincialism. The magnificent conception of the universe as seen through Buddhist eyes serves to emphasize the insignificance of our little personality, the purposelessness of evolutionary progression, and the hopelessness of aspiring to a heaven where eternal happiness prevails. Whatever heavens there be—and there are many in our world view—there is not a one which is ultimately desirable as an abiding place, however favourably it may compare with earth conditions !

The value of such a view of the cosmic system lies primarily in that it prevents us from emphasizing the feeling of self, from regarding our little selves as centres of cosmic interest. Though it does not flatter our sense of self-importance, it certainly conduces to a healthy and sober view, considering the part we play in the scheme of things. It is in this point that the Buddhist cosmology excels that of all other religious philosophies in that it cuts from under our feet at the very outset the material with which we might be tempted to construct a temple dedicated to the worship of a deity in the image of man.

It is therefore of little importance indeed to ascertain whether the views expressed above are correct in detail; but it is all-important that the lesson such notions have to teach be conveyed to the human mind as a preparation for man's fitness to tread the Noble Middle Path. This lesson once learned will serve as a background against which the virtues of desirelessness and self-effacement stand out as beacon lights against a clear black sky, and he who has profited thereby will forever be free from the insistency of fanatical notions. He is now prepared, without regard for his own predilections concerning the arrangement of the universe and his part therein, to look the facts squarely in the face and to see things as they really are. He does not any longer bend all his intellectual powers towards trying to explain things in a way that will distort the facts of existence to his own aggrandizement.

The Subjective View: Having thus reacted upon secondary truth—an outline of the universe in its magnitude and principle—he can now be entrusted with truth of primary significance, namely that his universe, in all its extent, in so far as it touches him at all physically and psychically, is of his own making and is part and parcel of the constituency of his Self.

One of the speculations most urgently pursued by the mind of man when it becomes sufficiently independent to ratiocinate, is that of the beginning and the possible ending of the world. He desires to know what happens to the earth, to the solar system, to the entire universe; how it came into being; how it progresses; how it will come to an end. Many textbooks are extant dealing with these subjects, and though from a scientific standpoint explanations on this score are exceedingly interesting, from a philosophical point of view they have little practical significance. Buddhism in particular eschews such speculations, for they do not practically concern man in his endeavour to tread the Path. This earth of ours no doubt had a beginning and will have an end! So the solar system. So the cosmic system to which our planetary family belongs. So also that larger system in which our cosmic system is but an item. And so on indefinitely. The history of our solar family may be regarded as a model for the larger cosmic combination as well as for those of the infinitesimal atom worlds. Details may vary, but, on the whole, principles do not.

To what extent do we really touch this world of ours? To what degree are we aware of its existence? In what measure are we affected by or do we affect its course? It is these that are the fundamental questions, and having solved them we can more legitimately turn our attention to the scientific aspect of the matter. Science to us is subservient to philosophy: not philosophy to science! We seek Wisdom above all!

The question is often asked: "Does not the universe exist independently of us? Are we not a part of the universe, and does not the fact whether we are here or not make little difference to the world as a whole?"

In a previous chapter we have remarked that "whatever be the nature of what is outside of us, to us it becomes reality only in so far as we associate sensations with it," and that "all that we call matter, substance, is that which reaches us through our sensations". In other words, it is our sensations that build us our world, and that represent our self in a certain relation to that world.

Whether that means that our sensations actually construct that world to the extent that the world ceases to be with the cessation of our sensations, is a question difficult to answer. The point is that *to us* the world only has significance in so far as we sense it, and that as soon as we cease to sense, the world *to us* is no more. The Buddhist refers not to the world as such. Outside of human experience the world has not even speculative value. This is well expressed by the Buddha when he says: "The world arises where the six senses are," the sixth sense being the confluence of the other five, the mind.

It is, of course, obvious that this does not mean that nothing exists that we do not actually sense with the eye, the ear, the touch, the taste, or the smell. But it does mean that whatever sensation is brought home to us by any one of the five senses is used by the mental retina as basic material wherewith to interpret future experience, until finally we shall have built the mental structure that represents our world view. If I am told that there is a country somewhere in Africa bearing the name of Timbuctoo, it does not matter whether I have ever actually been there, nor whether I have ever convinced myself of the actual existence of the African continent. My very experience of the existence of my own country and of my own continent is a sufficient basis whereupon to construct my concept of another continent and of another country existing thereon. When I am told that it is inhabited by people of a darker hue than my own, the fact that I may never have seen such persons would not militate against my belief in the existence of such people. The material wherewith to construct such a concept is already available within the scope of my experience. To build my universe I use the material at my disposal, just as I can employ material of the same kind for the construction of buildings of the most varied architecture. When, therefore, I am told of the existence of other universes, and of heavens and hells of varied substance, attributes, and time units, if I wish to accept such statements and employ them for the construction of my world concept, the world I have thus constructed is still entirely dependent upon my sense experience concerning the parts I have employed in the combination.

Thus, when the Buddha says: "Now I declare unto you that in this fathom-long perishable body, with its perceptions and imaginings, are contained the world, the arising of the world, the cessation of the world, and the way that leads to the cessation of the world", we have no quarrel with Him: on the contrary, we begin to see the utter truth of this statement. In this way we can understand also that the arising or, if you like, the creation of the world loses its formidable aspect and need not be ascribed to any external source such as a creating deity, although the notion that the world *is* created by a deity who rules it according to his lights need not be rejected as a scientific proposition and may safely enter our world view. If it does, however, such a creating deity also becomes part and parcel of our world as constructed by our mind material, our imagination!

We may say that we are living in a dream world and that the Buddha's appeal is intended to awaken us from this nightmare. The dreams with which we are acquainted often are not less real to us than is our daily life. The only difference lies in the fact that we ever return to this waking dream of ours, taking it up more or less where we left it, whereas the dreams of our sleep life do not seem to have the same coherence. It may be, however, that there is such a coherence to our sleep life of which we are conscious only during that sleep life and that therein our daily life may show as little continuity as our dream consciousness shows during our waking hours. In other words, it may well be that normally our sense of continuity is only active upon that place of existence where we happen to find ourselves at the time.

To recognize that we are living in a dream world need not detract in any way from its reality. For that is real which is sensed as real, not that which is real in the abstract. Only the abstract is the unreal. So that, though we may agree with other prevailing philosophies when we say that we are living in a world of dreams, we differ from them in that we pronounce this dream world real. The fact that this is a dream world does not by any means make it less of a real world.

The aim of Buddhism is to recognize this dream reality, and to substitute for it not another dream reality as we would do by pursuing the process of evolution towards godhood, but that wakefulness wherein all illusion is destroyed and wherein only Truth remains. This is the state of Nibbana, the cessation of the nightmare of evolutionary existence. Just as by waking from a vivid dream our dream world has ceased to be, so by the attainment of Nibbana the world now so real to us ceases to be. Has that dream world actually ceased to exist since we awoke ? Obviously this is a futile speculation. It may be an actual world wherein we participated for the time being. Or again it may have been a self-constructed set of mental pictures that evoked emotions as keen as do the facts of the world to which we are accustomed. What does it matter ? We have awakened. The dream is over. We are living in a different world again and have to react to the impacts now impinging upon us.

Even so, little is gained by speculating upon whether, once we awake to Nibbana, our present world has ceased to exist. It may have and it may not. But one thing is certain, namely, that *to us* this world is no more, that it has been dissolved. Where is the snake that pursued us in our dream ? Whether it has been destroyed or whether we escaped from its coils is immaterial. As far as we are concerned the old dream world has been destroyed, has been dissolved.

Buddhism teaches us systematically how the process of awakening from this dream world to Nibbana may be accomplished. Its ethics are all aimed at that result. The ethics of Buddhism differ from other ethics in that they do not teach us to be good for the sake merely of being good. To the ethicist this, no doubt, constitutes a defect! To us, on the other hand, to be good without any aim other than being good is like the supposed woman's reason: "Because . . !" To live the life prescribed by Buddhist ethics is good because it has the awakening effect. To tread the Noble Middle Path implies the acquisition of the knowledge why we should live so and not otherwise. For by so living we awaken to the world of truth from that of dreams, from the world created by fear and perpetuated by fear to the fearless state, the Beyondless Security. By eliminating craving for existence through non-insistence upon self, by looking within instead of without, can we dissolve the world. Says the Buddha: "And what, Disciples, is the destruction of the world? Through the total remainderless destruction of the thirst for being arises the destruction of the impulse to exist; through the destruction of the impulse to exist arises the destruction of perpetuation; through the destruction of perpetuation arises the destruction of the necessity for rebirth; and through the destruction of the necessity for rebirth arises the destruction of decrepitude and death, of sorrow, lamentation, pain, misery and despair. After such a fashion comes about the destruction of the entire complex of sorrow. This is the destruction of the world!"

Thus it will be seen that the question of the creation of the universe and that of its ending as such do not play any part whatsoever in the Buddhist scheme of things! To speculate upon these questions is regarded as wholly unprofitable. "O Disciples, think ye not such thoughts as the world thinks: the world is everlasting, or the world is not everlasting; the world is finite, or the world is not finite. If ye think, O Disciples, thus think ye: This is suffering; thus think ye: This is the origin of suffering; thus think ye: This is the extinction of suffering; thus think ye: This is the Path to the extinction of suffering." And when an inquirer point blank desires to know whether the Buddha has expressed himself definitely concerning the finiteness or infiniteness of the universe, he is told by one of the wise disciples, no doubt with his tongue in his cheek: "The Exalted One has not revealed this. As it does not conduce to salvation, as it does not conduce to the holy life, to separation from the earthly, to the extinction of desire, to cessation, to peace, to knowledge, to illumination, to Nibbana, therefore has the Exalted One not revealed this." And to a similar inquiry addressed to the Buddha Himself by the youth Purna, the latter is being courteously reproved : "Illustrious youth, what I deal with are the questions of sorrow, its accumulation, its extinction, and the manner of its extinction. These truths I explain and analyze ; they constitute my field of endeavour. Therefore I exclude and ignore all irrelevant questions, all personal preferences, all details concerning rebirth, all idle and vain quests !"

DEITY

IT must not be supposed that, simply because Buddhism does not recognize an ultimate, changeless and absolutely perfect Being, it is therefore an atheistic system. On the contrary, there is no religion which so thoroughly has probed the God problem as has Buddhism, and which is so utterly permeated with a wholesome, commonsense God recognition. But Buddhism has divested the conception of Deity of all superstitious accretions that the undeveloped human mind has attached to this idea.

To the Buddhist the notion of a perfect Godhead cannot possibly be reconciled with an imperfect world of His creation, for whatever springs from a Being perfect must of necessity be perfect also, and cannot be marred by imperfections, not even merely apparent ones. The very fact that things *appear* imperfect calls for an explanation as to what causes the imperfection of this appearance. It is true that elaborate theological theories have been evolved trying to account for this very contradiction, but none of them have succeeded in doing so with any degree of success for the simple reason that the human mind, upon reaching maturity, does not brook missing, broken or impaired links in the chain of logical succession. To assume a Godhead Who is at once perfect and yet the Creator of an obviously imperfect world; Who is most benevolent, and yet permits unutterable cruelties both in the animal and in the human states; Who is omnipotent, and yet powerless or unwilling to eliminate the most diabolical physical and mental torture; Who is all-loving and yet is responsible for and rules over a world filled with hatred: to the Buddhist such an assumption simply means that it is a false and mistaken assumption, and therefore he does not assume this. Neither, however, does the Buddhist go to the other extreme and assume that, because he cannot accept the notion of a perfect Godhead, an omnipotent Deity, there is no God at all. In other words, he sees how things stand with God; he puts the Deity in His proper place in the scheme of things; and he reveres Him for what He has achieved, though that be not perfection!

To begin with, Buddhism, like any other religion, recognizes a hierarchy of beings, each class of a more advanced type than the stage below it, with evolutionary tendencies, so that each class merges into the one next above. The mineral, vegetable, animal and human kingdoms are stages in this hierarchy. Above the human kingdom we enter the regions of the angels, the archangels, etc., beings as much ahead of the human as the human is ahead of the animal.

When we find the classification of the gods quite in evidence in Buddhist literature, the gods referred to are the classes belonging to this hierarchy above the human kingdom, or rather those who are the rulers of these classes, just as we would speak of the division of the nations of the earth into so many nationalities each with its president or king, or as we might refer to the eagle as the king of birds or to the lion as the king of beasts. Then, when we read say of the heaven of the thirty-three gods, we know we have to do with a region which has thirty-three subdivisions, each one of which ruled by or in charge of one of these thirty-three deities.

But there is a further concept connected with the god regions that it is of importance to understand and that is that we human beings are in much closer touch with their inhabitants than is generally realized. As entire departments of nature, such as the growth of plants, the distribution of insects, sections of animal life, their variations and adaptations, really are in charge of these devas—that is the inhabitants of the god regions—and of their rulers, we can readily see how, by thinking oɪ, praying to, and even sacrificing to beings connected with such activities, we may induce them to exert themselves in our favour, just as a petition offered to a king may direct his attention to the specific needs of the petitioner. And just as frequently the petitioners may never see their king face to face, so the believers in certain hierarchical chiefs of departments of nature may never come actually into touch with the latter, and only their thoughts impelled by desire reach them. Some, however, actually do approach these beings more closely and become consciously aware of their existence and of their power. But just as the non-believer will not attribute any value at all to such prayers and petitions, so the believer is apt to exaggerate the possibility of favourable response.

Now beliefs such as these are held by Buddhists as much as by adherents of any other religion. The main difference is that Buddhism not only sets forth these facts most clearly, but also deprecates the exercise of prayer and of sacrifice, as both of these acts are rooted in desire which in its turn is rooted in emphasis upon self. There is never any doubt expressed in the Buddhist scriptures as to the possibility of response to prayer or sacrifice. The point to be emphasized, however, is that, since our kamma will bring about the exact conditions at any time that we have ourselves prepared in the past, we but entangle ourselves the more and create fresh kamma by such practices: we add more fuel to the fire of craving!

Now it may also be true that we do not in all cases directly turn to the Great Being in charge of a department of nature—be its nature physical, emotional, or mental—but direct our prayers to what we consider the Ultimate Godhead. But Nature being, so to speak, divided into certain departments, it is obvious that any prayer having reference to that particular department will by its very nature immediately reach the Being it concerns, without carrying even to the greater Being in charge of our entire solar system. It is only the ignorance of the petitioner that makes him suppose, in case his prayer proves productive of results, that it has been answered by the Godhead Himself.

It is undoubtedly true that, in mentioning this subject, we are treating of high and powerful entities, at any rate from the human standpoint. But it is also true that relatively speaking we must not lose sight of their limitations. The average man constitutes but a factor in their calculations, whereas the awakened man, the man who has resolved to tread the Noble Path indicated by the Buddha, may entirely withdraw himself from the sphere of their power and influence, even from that of the highest amongst them. For not even the highest amongst the Gods has attained Nibbana, though He may be and perhaps is making such efforts as correspond to His station to attain it, just as a man may make such efforts in that direction as correspond to his. The lever which man provides the gods to make of him but an instrument in their evolutionary schemes is craving, whether it be craving of a high or of a low order. By the elimination of craving we cease to be mere tools and become truly free. It is this freedom which is referred to so frequently and so insistently in the Buddhist scriptures. "Hale we are amongst the ailing; we are free amongst the fettered; filled with love in a world of hatred; we have become feeders on rapture!" sings the Arahat, the Liberated. For He has been liberated from the necessity of rebirth either in this world or in any other, whether it be immediately after His decease or millions of ages hence. He has subtracted Himself from the sum total of the slaves bound by the Gods in evolutionary chains of their own providing. He no longer has to do His share to "make the world go round", to participate and acquiesce in the pain, the suffering, the misery, the despair of those He has left. In fact, His very leaving has lightened and loosened the shackles with which the unfree are bound, even as a stick removed from a bundle of sticks tied together, loosens up the entire bundle, making it easier for the other sticks to be removed. He has left *in order to loosen the shackles of his fellow men*, since all His love, all His sympathy, all His pity for their lot could not accomplish for them what His leaving could!

The greatness of the different God entities must not be minimized on the one hand, nor exaggerated on the other. Viewing their status from the average human stage of development, they are in many respects far beyond man in character, benevolence, co-operation, and intelligent sagacity. The departments of nature in their charge are administered as well as circumstances—including man's interference—will allow, and they count upon man's natural proclivities to aid them in the bringing about of certain physical, moral or racial results. But man, being a much more uncertain quantity than any of the other kingdoms of nature, nor being so co-operatively inclined especially at this epoch of history, frequently deflects the well laid plans of the deva regents, with the result that there is a great deal of confusion in the proper adjustment of things, and such confusion invariably redounds to the disadvantage of human society, particularly in that region where the proper co-operative spirit was not shown and where confusion was brought about in the first instance. To those of us living in the world, whether as yet they have decided to tread the Noble Middle Path or not, it is of great advantage to display a co-operative spirit, particularly co-operation with the so-called forces of nature, for that will bring about mutual understanding and good feeling between mankind and the kingdoms of the devas.

The lay Buddhist in all cases endeavours to bring about such good feeling. The result is that in Buddhist countries there is always manifest a joyful and co-operative spirit in regard to natural things. Where mechanical and industrial co-operation is concerned, however, which to some extent departs from natural law, we shall vainly look for its perfect operation in Buddhist countries. It may be said that the populace of Buddhist countries lives too closely in harmony with nature—that is with the prevailing devas—easily to lend itself to such a radical departure.

The monk follower of the Buddha, on the other hand, though recommending to the layman the promotion of co-operative harmony between him and the devas for the sake of kindliness and mutual prosperity, does not ally himself with the gods which he regards as the very beings who keep going the evolutionary treadmill. As it is his aim as quickly as possible to side-step the process of evolution, he naturally will not involve himself with the very forces that make for the conditions whence he wants to withdraw.

Nor must it be thought, however, that he opposes those forces. As already stated, if for any reason he is placed before the choice between helping the evolutionary forces or opposing them, he unhesitatingly will help them. But since his chief aim is to detach himself from everything that tends to keep him in evolutionary bondage, he will also detach himself from the forces in nature designed to keep the processes of evolution going.

In thus detaching himself he withdraws from the conflict of existence. For it must not be supposed that, simply because deva gods are in charge of departments in the economy of nature, these departments are running perfectly smoothly and automatically! On the contrary, the efforts on the part of these entities to bring about certain evolutionary results often are exceedingly strenuous and sometimes doomed to failure. Their activities are carried on in the face of great difficulties and even opposition on the part of other entities that have different ideas. There is as little unanimity amongst the gods as there is amongst mankind: the mythologies of all the religions testify to this. But whereas all other religions advise man to side with the conquering power—whether this power is good because it remained the stronger, or is stronger because it remained good, is a pertinent question—designating that conquering power God or good, and the opposing force Devil or evil; Buddhism tells man that it is possible to withdraw from this endless struggle. Were it ever settled finally, it would mean the end of the contesting parties, as Good and Evil are only so through contrast, through opposition. Buddhism is spiritual pacifism, based on the recognition of Kamma, on the recognition that whatever befalls us has been brought about by ourselves in the past and that to suffer it without complaint or protest is the quickest and safest way towards the eradication of craving, ill-will and self-insistence.

When the Buddhist therefore speaks of the God condition as an undesirable attainment, he does not do so because he looks askance at the God function or regards it as a fictitious function, but simply because it does not lead to that state of balance and of equanimity that is selfless and imperturbable. He realizes full well that the universe represents a divine victory: but he also realizes the strain and the cruelty attendant upon that victory. He recognizes that the hierarchical ranks, such as those of angel, archangel, etc., up to the God ruler are responsible and even comparatively pleasurable attainments accessible to him also in the course of time and evolution; but he also recognizes the futility of such attainment in the face of the larger quest, Nibbana! He thinks of these greater than human beings with respect and courtesy, with kindliness and good feeling; but he thinks of the Arahat, of the Noble One Who has attained, with a respect immeasurably greater and profounder than he can think of any God, however high the latter might have risen in the evolutionary free-for-all!

Thus the mature Buddhist has nothing to ask of even the greatest God. He knows that nothing can happen to him that he himself has not been instrumental in bringing about and that therefore he himself must be instrumental in removing.

Nor does he even ask the Deity's aid to that end. He depends upon his own courage, his own strength, his own endurance, his own intelligence, his own understanding, his own efforts, his own selflessness. What the Buddhist is striving for, Nibbana, is not in the possession of any God to bestow, for even a God, upon attaining Nibbana, must withdraw Himself from His world! Nor, for that matter, can the Buddha bestow it. But it was the Buddha who discovered that there *was* a way to complete liberation and who acquainted mankind with His discovery. The Buddha has bestowed upon mankind the knowledge of how to withdraw from between the pincers of Good and Evil, of God and Devil, of Criss and Cross. He has informed us that the highest morality consists not in taking sides in an endless fray, but in carrying kindliness and goodwill, love and understanding, sympathy and pity, to *all* without exception!

Does that mean that we must sit to one side and passively let things take their course? Does the nurse on the battlefield, though taking no sides, sit still and passive? Does he not display as much courage as the warrior, more sympathy, cooler self-sacrifice, more constant activity, greater helpfulness? So the follower of the Buddha in the conflict of the forces of existence recognizes no good side or evil side, no general, no commander. Himself not wanting anything, not even life temporary or eternal, he is mainly concerned with showing the way to spiritual peace to the combatants. But it is only among the wounded that the voice of the Buddha makes itself heard. Those who have not yet arrived at the realization that the Great Conflict is the cause of pain, misery, woe and unhappiness, that it is hopeless and endless, are not amenable to the words of the Peace Maker. They will fight on from life to life, now winning now losing, now elated now depressed, now of high rank now of low class, now rich now poor, now powerful now trod under heel; until finally they also will heed the Buddha's teaching or, if they have advanced themselves into the ranks of the Gods, the teachings of the Buddha corresponding to their own epoch. For though the Buddhas succeed each other as humanities succeed each other, Their teaching is essentially alike. But a Buddha's words can penetrate only to those who begin to understand that no permanent victory can be achieved in the struggle for existence.

The Buddhist's respect for the Gods in charge of the army groups is real, not feigned, for he knows by what superior qualities they must have attained their leadership. But he belongs to a different order of being, to an order making for balance rather than for weight on either scale, to an order that has no hierarchy, that is democratic in the extreme, that depends upon self-elimination instead of upon self-assertion. He belongs to the greatest brotherhood in the world, the Brotherhood of All That Lives. It was the Buddha who re-established this Brotherhood amongst mankind. It is the Sangha which has preserved for us the knowledge concerning the entrance to the Path of the Middle, the Path of Escape, the Path of Liberation from either Man-state or God-state, the Path of the Wise!

By this time it must be very clear to the reader of this treatise that Buddhism, though accepting the existence of a God, regards such God as holding the same relation to the other Gods of his own sphere of being as a man holds to other men of his social and intellectual status. And though it may be true that any God of that description may have charge of a universe so great that it passes human imagination, and over beings so numerous and multifarious that neither their number nor their kind can be grasped by the average human mind, it must never be forgotten that we ourselves are such Gods and that the universe in our charge—the human system—consists of an immense co-ordinated arrangement of cell systems each one of which comprises numerous molecular solar systems with all the appurtenances on their own scale of the other and next greater solar systems of which we are more in the habit of thinking, including time, space, cycles of evolutionary and devolutionary activity;

god, angel, man, animal, plant, mineral and elemental kingdoms.

At the same time it must ever be remembered that the Lord of our little solar system, however insignificant a system that may be in the scheme of things, to us holds the most significant relationship of loving Father to beloved children, wishing his children the best of luck in their individual kamma and dhamma, but unable seriously to interfere with them either for good or for evil. Kamma, the law universal of interactivity, and Dhamma, the understanding and application of that law, make it possible and necessary for each of us to work out our own salvation. To do so "with diligence" is the teaching of the Buddha, although it may be done gradually, so gradually, indeed, that it can hardly be said to be done at all. It is the fundamental idea of co-ordinated separateness, of interrelated individualism that is emphasized by Buddhism. Man, though a separate entity, holds the necessary relationships above, on his own level, and below, to all other separate individuals. As long as he insists upon that individual existence, whether on earth, in heaven, or in hell, such relationship is maintained with more or less friction, with greater or smaller difficulty, with higher or lower tension, with fiercer or milder pain. It is only when willing to renounce this individual insistency—not to melt it into a substratum of allness, a chimeric Absolute responsible for and connected with relative Manifestation, but to abolish all feeling and all notion of self in whatsoever form, particular or universal—that we can enter upon the Path to Salvation so ably and logically indicated by the Buddha.

Is this annihilation or not annihilation ? Will there be anything left or not ? Are we conscious of it or unconscious ? These are so many foolish enquiries that merely indicate our lack of understanding of the subject. If my watch runs down, where is the tick ? If I think of a window, do I first think of the room I look out of, or of the garden I look into ? If I burn a match, what will burn first, the width, the breadth, or the length ? Such questions as these are on a par with questions concerning the salvation of Nibbana. All that can be said about it is that it is a condition of timeless and utter happiness and bliss, aspired to by Gods and Men alike. And what more can be wanted ?

Now exactly what has to be accomplished by man has also to be accomplished by the Deity. He must attain Nibbana by entering upon the Path indicated by the Buddha. And each one of us human entities can more effectively help his God by entering upon the Noble Eightfold Path than by any other known method. To help the Deity in his evolutionary activities is laudable, for it must of necessity bring about a closer co-operation between God and men, besides producing pleasant kamma. But it also helps to keep alive the desire nature of both the Deity and oneself, with the result that the wheel is kept spinning, that the clock is kept wound, and that the forces of action and counteraction are kept at high tension. To enter upon the Middle Path, to endeavour to attain Nibbana, on the other hand, tends to create a balance between the opposing forces, it tends to peace human and divine, frictionless and beneficent, even and poised. Thus God is helped and also the world at large. As to oneself, one is helped also, perhaps more so, even: but what does that signify? It should be compassion for the world at large that makes us enter the Path, and not thought of Self. And as the Path is being trodden, so the world is being benefited, and the Treader of the Path gains the knowledge: "My treading the Path is benefiting the world, is diminishing suffering, is bringing liberation." And what is more worth while?

THE BROTHERHOOD

BUDDHISM teaches that there are two ways along which we may pursue existence. One of these ways, commonly called the evolutionary path, is the one taught by all the religions of the world, and they have in common the ethical foundations as also more or less definite instruction concerning a hierarchy of beings ranging from man to the very threshold of Deity. These teachings may differ in detail; the nomenclature may vary; their tendencies may change and adjust themselves to new and different human faculties; and they may even degenerate into superstitions and gather unethical excrescences. But, as can be easily verified by a study of comparative religion, at bottom they are identical in teaching the ascendant scale of divinities and in preaching ethical and moral conduct of a kind calculated to produce the quickest and the least painful advance from the human realm into the kingdom next above the human.

Now the Buddha considered that there were great numbers of human beings to whom the scheme of continuous and endless evolutionary progression could not appeal as a final solution of the problem of life. He considered that there must be a great number of human beings who felt, as He felt, that such a statement of the ultimate aim of existence was one of hopeless and heartless pessimism, offering no escape for the weary traveller as he climbed the evolutionary ladder rung by rung urged on by the glamour of new hopes and the promise of the fulfilment of new desires. It is true that the theory of at-one-ment, of union with the Absolute, might provide a satisfactory solution, but however far He looked, He could not discover this Absolute so urgently proclaimed by the adherents to the evolutionary scheme. That there was an urge towards progression, that there was an evolutionary advancement, step upon step and degree upon degree, could not be denied; that it lead from kingdom to kingdom, from glory to glory, was undoubtedly a fact. But as His vision acquired the range of this progression, as He discovered the motive underlying this tremendous and complex system within system, He also perceived that an Ultimate, an Absolute, was nowhere to be found, that it was as elusive as the horizon.

What the Buddha did discover, however, was that there was a loophole in this evolutionary chain; that it was possible to sidestep evolutionary progression; that there was a Path which, by keeping a mean between all extremes, led to a condition of such perfect balance that the urge to

* 14

advance, the desire to progress, the glamour of prospective glory, did not any longer act as a spur to the conquest of higher realms and of greater power. It was the discovery of this Path—the Noble Middle Path—which constituted Him the Buddha, the Wise One, the Teacher of Gods and of Men.

Having made this great discovery—unquestionably the greatest discovery ever made—the Buddha considered the advisability not only of acquainting mankind with the same, but also of gathering together into one body such human beings as were ready and willing to follow His example of putting His discovery to the test of personal experience, and thus the Sangha, the Brotherhood, the Order, was established. It was this Brotherhood which produced the Elders, those who reached the Goal of Balance, Nibbana; and the Path of the Elders is the Path that leads to the Goal they reached.

It may be said, therefore, that the Buddha taught two sets of teachings: not an exoteric and an esoteric set, as some would have it, but one set for those whose call it is to follow the evolutionary path, the Path of the Gods; and another for those who wish to attain Nibbana, the non-evolutionary Path, the Path of the Elders.

The early stages of the two Paths do not materially differ, except perhaps that in the Path of the Elders greater stress is laid upon the inherent suffering, pain, unhappiness, conciliation, transiency and evanescence that attaches to all activity, human and divine, in one way and another. The ethical precepts are the same, for in either case they lead out of the human kingdom : in the one instance to the kingdom next beyond the human ; in the other to the condition in which the disciple gathers the first fruits of the Path. The roads diverge where the adherent to the teachings of the Buddha becomes " converted ". Whereas the follower of the Path of the Gods continues his evolutionary pursuits, the follower of the Path of the Elders renounces evolutionary progress, centring all his efforts upon withdrawing from the evolutionary currents in which all other beings are swept onward. And it is at this stage that he can enter the Sangha and don the russet robe, its distinguishing mark.

The instructions of the Buddha to the laity, therefore, differ somewhat from those issued to His monastic disciples, for the former have not yet renounced the world, earthly and heavenly, whereas the latter already have taken the decision.

Thus if we consider the two great branches of Buddhism as they exist at the present day, namely that of the Hinayana, or Small Vehicle, and of the Mahayana, or Large Vehicle, we find that the Hinayana branch is virtually the Buddhism of the Elders, for it is the scheme of individual and non-evolutionary salvation through the attainment of Nibbana; whereas the Mahayana branch represents the scheme of collective evolutionary progression, depending upon the organization of humankind into one or more organs or portions of the larger Entity in Whom we live and move and have our being. This may ultimately lead to union with that Greater Entity, the conscious participation in His larger evolutionary activity; but it does not constitute ultimate salvation, it does not lead to the "Beyondless Security" associated with Nibbana.

This Greater Entity on his own level has all the attributes that we have in this sphere of existence, including the struggle for existence, the desire to live, the necessity of dying and of being reborn. And it is this His greater effort to maintain self-existence which in us reflects itself as our own effort to maintain *our* self-existence, even at the expense of each other. It is the Buddhist's aim to eliminate this selfish struggle by voluntarily giving up the self instead of artificially and forcefully maintaining it, enlarging it, or identifying it with a Greater Self built upon identical principles!

All the same, we must acknowledge the existence of this cosmic urge to conglomerate into a higher consciousness, and even indicate to those whose inclinations drive them in that direction the easiest and least offensive way to accomplish their desire, both for their own sake and for the sake of humanity at large. This indication constitutes the Mahayana branch of Buddhism. It corresponds with the aim of all other religions to point out the path to godhood and to educate mankind to tread the same through ceremonial, adoration, and prayer. So that we may say that there are really two religious movements in the world, namely, the Mahayana movement, comprising all ceremonial religions, more particularly in the present age Hinduism, Mahayana Buddhism, Roman Catholic Christianity, and Mohammedanism; and the Hinayana movement, exemplified only by the Path of the Buddha and the Buddhist Elders. Hence the extraordinary similarity in the ceremonial, the worship, and even the architectural details between the Mahayana Buddhist and the Roman Catholic religions. That they both have the same origin is not to be doubted; that that origin was Mahayana Buddhism is almost beyond dispute. Mahayana Buddhism and Roman Catholicism are two branches of the same faith, the faith that it is possible to accomplish union with the Deity; and they represent exactly the same method to attain that end. All the other world religions lead to the same goal: at-one-ment, yoga, union with the Deity, though they pursue somewhat different methods. All of them, however, are representative of the Mahayana movement, the Great or Collective Vehicle evolving towards godhood.

The Hinayana movement, on the other hand, is represented by Buddhism only, and that merely by the Buddhism of the Elders as it has come down to us through the ancient scriptures and as it has been preserved for us by the Brotherhood, the Sangha. The Sangha, therefore, is the body deponent of the teachings of the Buddha, which is one reason why in Buddhist countries it always has been regarded with particular affection and respect by the laity.

The layman holds a peculiar relation to the Brotherhood. He is given a set of ethical rules—not surpassed in beauty and comprehensiveness by the ethical admonitions of any other religion—together with the appropriate explanations *why* he should guide his actions thereby, and with the understanding that, if he lives in accordance with these precepts, he may, if he so wishes, leave the lay life and enter the life religious either temporarily or permanently as soon as his kamma permits. But the layman lives in the world and participates in its social, political, economic, commercial and professional arrangements, at the same time helping to improve as much as he can his environment in accordance with Buddhist recommendations. He endeavours to live the stainless and hurtless life and tries to persuade his fellows to do the same. He promises to heed the five admonitions: not to kill, not to steal, not to be unchaste, not to lie, and not to indulge in intoxicants; revering the Buddha as his Preceptor, the Dhamma as supplying the reason for heeding the precepts, and the Brotherhood as the vehicle deponent of the precepts. More than this the layman is not called upon to do. He can pursue his usual vocations and avocations, benefiting both as an individual and as a social unit to the extent that the precepts are followed by himself and within his community. And the history of the last 2500 years of the countries in which Buddhism has become the popular religion proves that the inhabitants of such countries are happy, contented, charitable, cheerful, courteous and devout, intelligent and artistic, sober and faithful.

The Order: On the other hand, the bhikkhu or monk whose purpose it is to follow the Path to Nibbana, entirely severs his connection with the world, except in so far as his religious duties bring him into contact with its inhabitants. Every free man may join the Brotherhood, either temporarily or permanently. The Sangha cannot be called an organization, for degrees of titles and power are virtually absent. Nor does it constitute an hierarchy involving dignities of graduated progression. Rather it is a democratic assembly in which every man rules himself in accordance with the Buddha's precepts. Whereas the layman merely promises to heed five admonitions, the bhikkhu promises to follow ten rules, which are: (1) Not to take life; (2) Not to take what is not voluntarily given; (3) To be chaste; (4) Not to lie; (5) Not to use intoxicating drink or drug; (6) To eat but once a day and that before noon; (7) Not to dance, sing, or play; (8) Not to wear ornaments or use cosmetics; (9) To sleep on a low, hard couch; (10) Not to handle money. He looks to the Buddha, the Dhamma, and the Sangha for his inspiration.

It will be noticed that, though the bhikkhu is bound to observe chastity and poverty, he does not vow obedience to any other being. In this respect the Sangha differs from most other religious orders and emphasizes its democratic character. The bhikkhus are not priests, no priesthood being sanctioned by the Elders: they simply form a democratic body of men bent upon leading the religious life in accordance with the Buddhist norm.

To enter the Order a man must be free, that is to say he may not be in the employ of king or government, he may not be in debt or dependent, he may not be diseased or deformed. If he cannot leave government employ, he may not be admitted: if he cannot settle his debts, he may not join until he has done so; if he is dependent, he must first be released by those on whom he is dependent; if he is sick he must recover first; if deformed, he must wait until another incarnation, for in this particular life his kamma evidently is too heavy. This of course does not mean that, should a Brother become ill or suffer a deforming accident whilst in the Order, he must resign or is expelled. On the contrary, the most tender care is bestowed upon him. But only freemen may enter the Sangha, and nothing may bind them to the world they have left. Those whose kamma is such that they cannot extricate themselves from debt; resign from a government post; free themselves from dependence; rid themselves of disease; or rectify their deformity, may be good lay Buddhists, but they cannot become incorporated in the Order during their present birth, for they are evidently working out incompatible kamma. If the remainder of this life suffices to satisfy their kammic debt they may, should they still wish to do so, enter the Sangha upon their return into physical existence.

He who dons the russet robe—the distinguishing mark of the Order—may return to the life of the world whenever he chooses, for his vows are binding only for so long as he remains within the Sangha. No religion so generously and adequately provides for the satisfaction of the urge to retire, if only temporarily, from the world with its vanities and profanities, its hurry and flurry, its push and pressure—a common experience to most human beings at some period of their life—as does Buddhism. And the temporarily retired is on exactly the same footing as the monk whose call it is to remain within the Order permanently, always allowing for seniority.

There is an intermediate state, however, that of the novice or temporarily retired, in which the first eight promises only are made and the last two, those providing for sleeping on a low and hard couch and for not handling money, need not be observed But the person who takes the eight observances only, has not really entered the Order and, as a rule, is only testing out the monastic life for the purpose of becoming acquainted with it and to see whether it happens to be the condition suited to him; or else he wishes to be in closer touch with the Brotherhood and to absorb some of its teachings more adequately than would be possible as a mere layman. He might as well hold to all ten observances if it were not that he is merely intending to live in retirement for a short time, say for a week or two, or even less, for which reason his mental efficiency might become impaired by sleeping in an unaccustomed fashion and his worldly interests be damaged by keeping aloof from business transactions in cases of emergency.

The Monk's Training: Upon entering the Order the new monk is placed under the superintendence of a senior Brother whose duty it is to acquaint his charge with the detailed regulations governing the monk's food, clothing, and housing, and who is responsible for their observance by the new member. He must see to it that he makes and dyes and washes his garments in accordance with the requirements; that he attends to the sanitation and ventilation of his quarters: that he properly cleans and suns the furniture, objects, and articles in the habitation; etc. Although too great a degree of comfort is not tolerated and all luxuriousness avoided, at the same time no severely ascetic practices are allowed and sufficient scope is left for the expression of individual predilections.

It will be clearly seen from the above that the Buddhist monastic life is not by any means one of severe asceticism. Above all, it must be fully realized by those interested in this subject that no accusation of outward uncleanliness can be levelled against the bhikkhu. Such writers as have been endeavouring to picture the Buddhist monk as a man lazy and self-sufficient, or unclean in his habit and attire, must be branded as either ignorant or malicious. The prescriptions are detailed and clear: outward cleanliness must accompany inward purity.

The Path the bhikkhu is travelling does not permit his engaging in any creative activity whatsoever. He may not exercise the sex function; till the soil; produce or help produce crops; do physical labour other than what is essential for the sanitation of his quarters; go errands for laymen, even though they be princes or kings ; engage in the arts ; or pursue *for their own sake* any of the sciences. His line of activity is entirely confined to the study and verification of Buddhist philosophy and psychology, the purification of the heart and of the mind, and the practice of the exercises of concentration, meditation and ecstasy : in other words, it is decreative. His sole purpose is to tread the Path, to withdraw himself from the evolutionary scheme of things, and to attain Nibbana.

We must enlarge a little upon these various restrictions and explain why they are prescribed.

The man who exercises the sex function immediately places himself within the swirl of those cosmic forces that have to do with procreation and continuance. The bhikkhu tries to get away from these forces and to place himself outside of this current. The sex act emphasizes existence and produces the kind of kamma which, by tending to bring other beings into this world, causes him in return to be brought again into physical life. By refusing to remain a party to this endless chain of producing and being produced, he may break away from this cosmic current, and finally cross the stream of existence.

The bhikkhu may not till the soil for the reason that by so doing he places himself under obligation to those devas who are connected with the reproductive processes of nature. Although such a tie is not quite so binding as the one governing human procreation, yet it is one of those that have to be severed. The bhikkhu for his maintenance relies entirely upon the householders of neighbouring communities. Every morning, carrying the food bowl before him, he passes through the village, halting at each door and waiting to receive some food in his bowl. He is not permitted in any way to call the attention of the inhabitants to his presence. If he receives nothing, he passes on to the next dwelling. If something is put into his dish, he continues to the next house, and so on until his bowl is filled or until such time as will enable him to return to his quarters and eat the contents before noon. This constitutes his only daily meal. The bhikkhu must be satisfied with what he obtains, may not halt at such houses only where he is sure to get food omitting those where he usually receives little or nothing, but must take each house in the order as he reaches it. He neither expresses thanks where he receives, nor disapprobation where he does not. Since in Buddhist communities it is esteemed a privilege by the lay householder to be permitted to put some food into the bhikkhu's bowl, however little, the monk as a rule is sufficiently well fed. If he does not finish the contents of his bowl, he may not lay aside the the remainder for the morrow. He may, however, share his food with those of his fellow monks who have fared less well in their morning rounds than he has. In return for his scant support the monk at all proper times is accessible to the layman who desires instruction, which fact is regarded as cancelling the obligation incurred. Since most laymen intend sooner or later to enter the religious life themselves, when they also will have to obtain their support similarly, they are not likely to let the bhikkhu go by without contributing at least some food for his support, unless indeed they are so poor that they cannot even spare a mouthful. The one exception to the above regulations consists in the bhikkhu being permitted to accept invitations to eat at a layman's house, in which case, at the conclusion of the meal, he pronounces a religious discourse fitted to the understanding of his hearers. This cancels his obligation.

The bhikkhu may not engage in the arts, since by so doing he again stimulates his creative faculties in the direction of materializing form, colour, or sound. Such activity also is connected with the pursuits of certain classes of devas, and pertains to the evolutionary path. He does not deprecate the pursuit of sculpture, painting, or music among the laymen. On the contrary, he commends it for those whose call is this evolutionary line of progression, for it is a legitimate channel along which to divert the lower creative impulses, although it remains understood that the development of artistic expression as such is a hindrance on the Path to Nibbana.

Nor may the bhikkhu pursue any of the sciences *for their own sake*, for the reason that doing so diverts his mind from the great issue at hand. To gather facts may be an interesting pastime, it may systematize the mentality, it may illustrate and even discover important theories, but from the Buddhist point of view only such facts are of value as aid in elucidating the problems of its philosophy, that have a bearing upon the elimination of the self, that lead to disentanglement and to liberation: in other words, the facts that are essential. For example, the collecting of shells or beetles and their classification, a scientific enough pursuit, is regarded as a mere game which, with other games, is not to be indulged in. It is told of the Buddha that, when passing through a Jeta thicket with a retinue of monks at a time when this very topic was under discussion and when the autumn leaves lay thickly on the ground, the Buddha picked up a handful of leaves and, addressing his monks, asked: "What think ye, O Monks, is more, the leaves I hold in my hand or those still lying upon the ground in this Jeta thicket?" "The leaves still lying upon the ground in this Jeta thicket, Sire, are more". "Thus, O Bhikkhus, are the facts at the disposal of the Buddha more than those actually required for the gaining of liberation." This attitude, however, must by no means be misconstrued. It does not signify that newly discovered facts should be disregarded. It merely means that no undue attention should be bestowed upon unessential and impertinent discoveries, such as, for example, the method in which a winnow uses its tail, or the exact calculation of the magnitude of Betelgeuze, or the time it may take for a pin to become rusty in a given temperature at a given moisture!

The entire attitude of the bhikkhu is that of a man seeking deliverance by his own efforts. His liberation is not encompassed by the Buddha. The teachings of the Wise One are only for the purpose of enabling His followers to liberate themselves, even as the Buddha succeeded in liberating Himself. The Buddha's statements are accepted not simply because He enunciated them, but because their inherent accuracy becomes clear to the mind of the disciple and can be verified by him in every particular sooner or later. Says the Buddha: "If ye know thus and see thus, O Bhikkhus, will ye therefore say: We respect the Master, and out of reverence for the Master do we thus speak?" "That we shall not, Sire." "What ye speak, O Bhikkhus, is it not even that which ye have yourselves known, yourselves seen, yourselves realized?" "Thus it is, Sire!."

It must also be clearly understood that Buddhism, besides acknowledging no revelation, by the Buddha's own words is not even dependent upon the acceptance of the teachings of the Founder. Says the Buddha to Ananda, his cousin and closest disciple: "Whosoever now, Ananda, or after my departure, shall be his own light, his own refuge, and shall seek no other refuge; whosoever taketh the Truth as his light and his refuge and seek no other refuge, such henceforth, Ananda, will be my true disciples who walk in the right path." If any truth can be found not consistent with the Buddha's teaching, it is the Buddha's express wish that it be followed in preference to His own teaching! But it must also be acknowledged that in the course of the 2500 years that have elapsed since the emancipation of the Wise One, no such truth has made its appearance! In the formula so frequently quoted: "I take my refuge in the Buddha; I take my refuge in the Dhamma; I take my refuge in the Sangha," the word "refuge" is a mistranslation. Only the Truth as he perceives it is the Buddhist's refuge. But on becoming a Buddhist, and on other solemn occasions, we remind ourselves that we look to the Buddha as the Discoverer of the Path leading out of evolutionary progression; that we look to the Dhamma as the presentation of that Path; that we look to the Brotherhood as the Body Deponent, the Guardian, of the Teaching concerning this Path. But refuge we take only in the Truth!

The training of the Monk is divided into three parts. In the Buddha's words: "There are three trainings, Bhikkhus. Which are the three? *The*

Higher Ethics: when a bhikkhu lives by the code of discipline and in conformity with the ethical precepts; *The Higher Consciousness*: when a bhikkhu, aloof from sense appetites, aloof from evil thoughts, enters into and abides in the four states of ecstasy in succession; *The Higher Insight*: when a bhikkhu knows as it really is that "This is ill; this is the cause of ill; this is the cessation of ill; this is the Way leading to the cessation of ill!" These three trainings are not different in kind. Rather, they are successive in character. The first part trains the monk in behaviour, the second in experience, the third in understanding. For real understanding cannot be had without experience, just as experience cannot be obtained in sufficient degree without leading the ethical life and removing the obstructions induced by sense desire and attachment.

The above is a most interesting division. In the first training or discipline the monk is enjoined to rid himself of the three poisons of covetousness, anger, and delusion, as well as the tendencies thereto, for it is these three that are at the bottom of all suffering, animal, human, and divine! But realizing that there is suffering; realizing that craving is the cause of suffering; realizing that he must abolish craving in order to abolish suffering; he must yet learn that he *can* rid himself of craving. Now the Buddha and His Arahats maintain that it *is* possible to eradicate all craving, all longing, all urgent desire, by means of treading the Noble Path. Stretching a point, this may be said to constitute the only Article of Faith of the Buddhist. Only he who successfully is treading the Noble Path can change this faith into knowledge, for he gains the requisite experience in the second training, and finally the requisite insight in the third. He changes covetousness into detachment; anger into love: and delusion into knowledge. The final insight to which he attains resolves itself into three factors: impermanence, evil, not-self. The impermanent nature or evanescence of things, the inherent evil or undersirableness of things, the absence of a fundamental self or underlying unity in things, have to become an habitual attitude of mind on the part of the trained bhikkhu. It is only when he has achieved this that he can be of sound judgment, that he has a reliable basis for the understanding of the true nature of himself and the world about him. Socrates' adage "Man, know thyself" to the Buddhist sounds: "Man, recognize thy non-self!"

The democratic nature of the Sangha was emphasized by the period in which it was established. The social system at the time of the Buddha was based upon the maintenance of the four castes of Kshattriyas or Warriors, Brahmans or Priests, Vaishyas or Merchants, and Shudras or Labourers. These castes were strictly adhered to and, as a rule, birth decided definitely the caste of the person born. Great pride of caste prevailed, especially in the higher ones, and to renounce caste was tantamount to social ostracism. Notwithstanding, the man entering the Sangha had to renounce caste unconditionally, for no distinction of caste was tolerated in the assembly of bhikkhus. In the Sangha all had to be on the same initial level, "as the great streams, O Disciples, however many they be, when they reach the great ocean, lose their old name and their old descent, and bear only one name, namely 'the great ocean'."

The regard in which the Sangha was held is well indicated by the King Ajatasattu's reply to the Buddha's question. "If a slave or servant of the king puts on the yellow robe and lives as a monk without reproach in thought, word, and deed, wouldst thou then say: Let this man still be my slave and servant, stand in my presence, bow before me, take upon himself to perform my behests, live to minister to my pleasures, speak deferentially, hang upon my word?" To which question the king answers: "No, Sire, I would bow before him, stand before him, invite him to sit down, give him what he needed in the way of clothing, food, shelter, and of medicine when he is ill, and I should assure him of protection, watch and ward, as is becoming." The Buddha, Who Himself was a prince, regarded "the dignities of kings and princes as the dust motes in the sun beam; the value of gold and silver as that of a broken platter: the collective chiliocosm as the first letter of the alphabet; the various forms of manifest existence as the changes of vegetation during the four seasons: but the state of perfect mental equilibrium as the true standing ground!"

The impersonal nature of the Buddha with regard to His teaching is well exemplified by his reply to Ananda, His cousin and personal attendant, when the latter asked the Buddha who would take His place as a leader and teacher after His passing away. "It may be, Ananda, that some of ye will think: The word of the Teacher is a thing of the past; we have now no Teacher. But that, Ananda, is not the correct view. The Dhamma and the Discipline, Ananda, which I have taught and enjoined upon ye is to be your Teacher when I am gone." And with regard to the teaching of His Doctrine, the Buddha said: "Any monk, O Monks, who in teaching the Doctrine to others thinks as follows: 'The Doctrine has been well taught by the Blessed One, avails even in the present life, is immediate in its results, is inviting and conducive to salvation, and may be mastered by any intelligent man for himself. O, that they may hear from me the Doctrine, and be enlightened by what they hear, and as a result of their enlightenment begin to act accordingly!' and who thus teaches the Doctrine to others because of that Doctrine's intrinsic goodness, and because of compassion, mercy, and kindness: such a monk, O Monks, is a worthy teacher of the Doctrine."

The Buddha frequently referred to the superiority of the Brother well advanced along the Path of the Elders over the God well advanced along the Path of Evolution: "Sakka, foremost amongst the Gods (of the Heaven of the Thirty-three), O Monks, is not free from passion, not free from dislike, not free from attachment; is not released from birth, decrepitude, death, sorrow, lamentation, misery, grief, and despair; in short, he is not released from ill!" whereas the Arahat is so released. And that His aim was far from attaining to any heaven no matter how high, is well exemplified by His admonition to His followers: "If members of another religious sect, O Monks, were to ask you: Sirs, is it in order to attain to the world of the Gods that the Monk Gotama leads a holy life? would ye not, O Monks, if that question were put to you, be distressed at, ashamed of, and discomfited by the very idea?"

Magic: It has been hinted in the foregoing pages that the bhikkhu who is well advanced along the Path of the Elders acquires faculties of consciousness and investigation not possessed by ordinary humans. Yet it must be emphasized that the acquirement of such faculties may not play any part in inducing a person to enter the

Sangha. Clairvoyance, clairaudience, levitation, communion with spirits, devas, and other superphysical beings, is not taught, nor is such acquirement encouraged. If such powers be acquired, however, as they frequently are, it is purely incidental and no display of them is permitted or tolerated. Disregard of this injunction may result in expulsion from the Order. The monk who acquires any of these powers may himself employ them only for purposes of verification and liberation : never for display or even to convince or convert others. Nor may such faculties be used for the prolongation of life or for other acts of magic. The abuse of such faculties and powers is practised, for example, by those "who make use of specially prepared food for the purpose of perfection ;" "who study the virtues of trees, plants, and herbs to perfect themselves in the use of medicine and potions to inhibit normal faculties and produce abnormal ones ;" "who by incantations are able to alter their condition at will ;" "who by the practice of concentration perfect their memory and reconstruct the past or preconstruct the future ;" "who by sudden intervention remove difficulties in human affairs ;" "who acquire enlightenment by a thorough study of the system of changes and conversions in nature." "All such may attain various degrees of supernormal knowledge or extend their lives to a thousand or a myriad years. Dwelling in mountains or islands, beyond the habitations of men, they practise their various modes of life. Notwithstanding, they are still involved in the wheel of birth and death and are not depending upon the true method of emancipation. For after their term is expired they must return again to the various forms of beings that are involved in the net of existence." In other words, if any such powers be acquired, such acquisition must be incidental, not deliberate and intentional; and if any such faculties are used, they must be used for permanent liberation and not for the purpose of practising magic, for the extension of existence, for self-aggrandizement, or for interfering or intervening in the affairs of men or of the world. They must be simplifying, not complicating. There is but one legitimate aim that the bhikkhu may pursue, and that is liberation in Nibbana, the only permanent and abiding liberation possible.

From the foregoing it will be seen that the life of the bhikkhu is a serious and carefully premeditated proposition: that it is full of activity but that there is little room for any other pursuit than the specific one for which the monastic life has been entered upon. The monk is continually training himself to be subdued and meditative, to be awake and mentally active, to be helpful and courteous. Nor may he lose touch with those who still lead the life of the layman. The monastic life is not to be adopted lightly, for which reason in some Buddhist countries all young men pass through the Order so that in later life, when they may feel called upon to become monks, they may fully realize their duties and obligations. Although not extremely ascetic, as asceticism goes in the East, the life of the Buddhist monk is far from inviting except to those whose purpose is set and serious. And the laity, appreciating this, will ever respect and assist those who have left the life of the world to seek final liberation amongst the Treaders of the Noble Eightfold Path amongst the members of the Buddhist Brotherhood—the Sangha. Blessed is that country where the Order is allowed to flourish !